A NINETEENTH-CENTURY CHILDHOOD

A
NINETEENTH-CENTURY
CHILDHOOD

BY

MARY MacCARTHY

WITH AN INTRODUCTION
BY
JOHN BETJEMAN

HAMISH HAMILTON
LONDON

First published, 1924
Included in New Adelphi Library, 1929
New Edition, 1948
Second Impression, February 1949

Printed in Great Britain by
Ebenezer Baylis and Son Ltd. The
Trinity Press, Worcester, and London

DEDICATED
TO
DESMOND MACCARTHY

ILLUSTRATIONS

INTRODUCTION

BOOKS about a world remote from the present often take some reading. Not this one though; alas, it is all too easy to read! The style has an insinuating charm. Through it blows the scent of dried rose petals in the blue bowl on a drawing-room table; the crack of the croquet mallet, the plash of the punt pole, the crunch on gravel of a visitor's carriage are heard in its pages: as evening falls, the tones of a church bell sound across the misty sunset elms and strike the still small note of the Christian Religion into the work-a-day air. Be warned against the witch's style. Be warned! You may read its melodious sentences aloud to friends in your functional flatlet. Not the chromium, nor the steel chair, nor the newest number of the newest periodical will be proof against those swift-flowing sentences. You will all be caught in their waters and drowned.

A solitary reading of it will drown you deeper than ever. For this is a fatally short book and can be finished in an hour-and-a-half. To several of us is still allotted an hour-and-a-half in the week to ourselves. This book is short because it is like a lyric and, like all perfect lyrics, it would be spoiled if one word were added to the perfection of its brevity. One hour-and-a-half's reading! But the effect of that short time will remain in the mind for years.

Well may the reader inquire, 'But why so much fuss? And why this portentous warning? This book,

I have heard, was originally published in 1924. It is the autobiography of a woman who was a girl at the end of the last century. She and her brothers and sisters lived then at Eton where their father was Vice-Provost and their mother a charming social figure. For all that, few well-known names appear in the book. Besides, it all ends with the death of Queen Victoria, the date when the old order disappeared and the authoress was still a young girl incapable of mature judgment. So why so much fuss? I do not see how the book can be different from many other volumes of nostalgic reminiscence.'

And the answer to all that is, that it *is* different. *A Nineteenth-Century Childhood* is an exceptional book. There have indeed, been many volumes of reminiscence of those times. Some are written from the point of view of 'those were the days, and everything is now much worse.' There is a note of self-pity in their pages, a whine for lost complacency. Others are written in order to put in as many famous names as possible, with second-hand or even first-hand stories attached to each. An ample index is furnished at the end. But *A Nineteenth-Century Childhood* would look ridiculous with an index. As well index Coleridge's *Ancient Mariner*! Yet other books are written in support of some social theory, some æsthetic or political creed. This book was written for none of these reasons.

It is the product of reverence and affection, reverence for home life and love for the family, its dwelling places, its servants and surroundings. Obviously it was inspired. The authoress wrote it as a true poet writes true poems, not for self-glory or money but

10

for love of doing it and for recording moments of full-life and happiness. Above everything, this book shows the happiness of a family life when the family consists of whole, untwisted people with a standard of behaviour in common and all the resources of literature and the arts, jokes, enjoyable conversation, outdoor life and town life theirs for the asking.

A book becomes, I think, a work of genius when something is infused into it from outside, without the author, at the time of writing, being aware that this is happening. If this is true, then *A Nineteenth-Century Childhood* is a work of genius. Mrs. MacCarthy's delight in English is as great as her delight in that sunny, cedar-shaded childhood she is recording. Unpretentiously she makes full use of the rhythms and varied periods which only a skilled writer of English prose can employ. There is nothing consciously 'beautiful' about her prose, but it seems to have a rhythm or rather a series of rhythms, of its own. Sometimes she writes in a matter-of-fact way, interrupts with conversation, sometimes she sails into Victorian sunlight and the reader sails with her, scarcely aware whether he is reading or really taking part in the scenes before him. With unerring dexterity she knows when to walk, when to soar, when to stop and talk, when to run, so that the quiet journey is always varied.

She has concentrated, deliberately, on the pleasures of her childhood. Such a subject might be a vapid one for a book. So would this have been, were it not for just the quality that gives it genius.

Wrapping round the little pleasures of her childhood, enlivening even the reflective paragraphs, is a

11

golden light from outside. The book lives in the sunset glow from a settled order of things. There has been no need for her to emphasize the twelve roaring fires to which servants carried coals in winter, nor to question the extravagances, as they now seem, of household management. Those who were born to live a sequestered life in the family of a scholar and a gentleman took such things for granted, as they took for granted, the stable-scented carriage-drawn world outside and the liberal intellectual talk round the table at home.

Mrs. MacCarthy's family was undoubtedly Liberal in sentiment, though not, I should fancy, Radical. One might discuss from the soup until the port schemes for social improvement and equal opportunities for all. Rather more opportunities were afforded to the talented in those days than is generally supposed. But the fact remains that there was a settled order of things in England from the Queen upon the throne to the servants in the basement and it must have seemed that nothing short of a miracle would dislodge it. The miracle was two world wars.

Mrs. MacCarthy is aware that this order was largely taken for granted in the eighteen-eighties and that it was nearly dead and mocked and despised by 1924. Without more than the gayest, lightest, kindest comparison of those days with the present, she has given the book the authentic atmosphere of its time. Perhaps it would be more accurate to say the book has, from outside, been given the atmosphere of its time. And this raises it from the ink-smell and the paper-smell of so many autobiographies to the rarer air of literature. This is the gift of genius.

On the surface *A Ninteeenth-Century Childhood* is a charming, direct and gay account of a sheltered childhood fifty and more odd years ago. If it were only that, it would be one more 'charming' book by a lady writer. But around that gaiety and pleasure, there is a calm which is profound. This calmness, the genius of the book, comes, as I have said, from the spontaneous reverence and charity with which it is written. It is born of a desire to catch a bright facet of Eternity and to record it in Time.

JOHN BETJEMAN

February, 1948

AUTHOR'S NOTE

IN the original edition of this book places and people were given fictitious names; but in this reprint a quarter of a century later I have given the real names Windsor and Eton in the place of fictitious 'Camelot' and 'Runnymede,' above all the real 'Vice-Provost of Eton' in the place of the fictitious title 'The Warden.' But my family particularly desired that their own Christian names and surname should be fictitious in the book. I have therefore obediently retained the invented Christian names, and the surname 'Kestell,' and have refrained from portraits of all save the back view of my father, the Vice-Provost.

CHAPTER ONE

I was born in the 'eighties into a sheltered, comfortable, religious, and literary circle.

Politics to this *milieu* seemed harmless and diverting matters for academic dispute. Politicians were then noble gentlemen unpaid, and a Conservative was then a Conservative and a Liberal a Liberal. The earliest election I can remember seemed to be a game with an old gentleman called Lord Salisbury climbing up a ladder every morning in the *Times*, neck and neck with an old gentleman called Mr. Gladstone on another ladder, who finally reached the top rung first.

Poetry, as we know, was then uplifting and romantic. The Poet Laureate, Lord Tennyson, was living a deliciously sheltered life at Farringford, perplexed about immortality on the windy downs.

In art, as in poetry, an orgy of parable, intense symbolism, and legend was being enjoyed in the works of the Pre-Raphaelites; William Morris's chintzes and wallpapers had been accepted, and his Socialism left quietly at Hammersmith. As for religion, the Oxford Movement was over. Tolstoi's devastating pamphlets had not yet been translated into English; the vagueness of Mr. Jowett's sermons was welcome to all.

Satan is said to have guffawed with incredulity till Hell echoed when an angel came to tell him that St. Augustine had converted England. It is the solemn sense of salvation in each generation that makes matter for cynicism. If I have just now appeared to chime in with the devil's yells with a faint yet presumptuous titter, let me hasten to say that it is with full consciousness that this *present* age of culture, confusing brutality with sincerity, and duped by madmen or charlatans, will be under the lash of the next generation's laughter in no time.

Well, a memoir is a trap for egotism: I have nibbled the cheese, I am snapped in; a wretched mouse quivering with self-importance and destined for immediate drowning.

By my father I am exclusively West Country English; by my mother I am lowland Scottish. My father's family have been settled in Devonshire ever since the sixteenth century, and have always been very quiet, mild people. The bones of these small squires, ensigns in line regiments, lieutenants of marines, and scholarly country clergymen, lie buried in their own corners of that sleepy county. They were careful of family records from earliest times, and some of their wives came of ancient and picturesque families of Somerset, Cornwall, and Devon. I myself would like to linger among these old skeletons, but I will not; for records are very interesting to a descendant, but hardly a matter of curiosity to the general reader.

My maternal grandfather (Scottish) had died in India at the age of forty-six, eminent, and leaving a good fortune. My grandmother settled down after his death in a country house in the West of England with her sons and daughters. I have visited this house in later days with my mother; and, as, without ringing the bell, we stood on the steps looking into the quiet hall, she a ghost returned in the company of the living, I could see the picture she described: I could see her and her sisters flitting up and down the wide staircase in white muslins, with camellias in their hair and Beethoven scores under their arms.

Their life there seemed to be made of many moonlight picnics, much croquet and claret cup on the lawn, opera singing and waltzing. They went up to London for delicious parties; they had a glorious *culte*, Lord Tennyson, at Farringford.

We stood for a long time looking in at this silent house. Then we walked round by the conservatory, from which they picked the camellias for their hair; and, as we crossed the lawn, my mother told me about the *culte* for Tennyson and their visits to him. She called up herself and her sisters out of the past once more, this time at the poet's home, Farringford, in the Isle of Wight, sitting round a shining mahogany table under candles, with wine and fruit before them, spellbound by the bard's conversation.

It was in this country house that my father fell in love with my mother when she was seventeen, in her white muslin, with her pink camellia in her hair and her Beethoven score under her arm! By the time she was eighteen she was married to him. I was the seventh child of their family of eight.

Though brought up to believe ourselves gravely poor, it seems to me by the light of later adversity that we were either quite rich or gravely extravagant. At least twelve fires roared up twelve chimneys all day, all the winter through, in our house at the great public school, Eton, where we lived. I can hear the coal being shovelled and shot and poured and heaped

17

on by servants, at intervals throughout the day; my mother even had two fireplaces, filled with red-hot coals, in her long large bedroom, to muse by. A whole legion of those easily procured nineteenth-century servants filed in to family prayers daily. Housemaids, with print skirts that stuck out and crackled with starch in a manner that has died out, called people all over the house in the morning with innumerable trays of tea, and with heavy bath-cans of scalding water, which they had carried up stair-cases and along endless lengths of passages – just as in the evening they carried moonlike globe lamps everywhere to light up the old labour-making house – with the unmurmuring and unquestioning good-will of those comfortable days. Twice a year the whole household, numbering about fifteen souls, with about twenty trunks, was transported as a matter of course by rail to our country home in the most remote corner of Devonshire, twenty miles from a railway station.

A governess taught the schoolroom party, a nurse and nursemaid undertook the nursery, leaving my mother free for reverie by her fires; our brothers went to the most approved private schools, and after-wards to Eton, Winchester, and Sandhurst. They hunted in the holidays; and there was much journey-ing to London, or to Italy, or to France. And yet my indulgent and generous father, usually in a state of financial agitation, could never see where he could cut down one single expense, and always spoke as if we were all herded in a garret and did not know where to turn for bread.

Our home at Eton was a flat-roofed, rambling,

18

yellow-brick house with a balcony, and a magnolia tree climbing up its walls on the garden side. Let us see a picture of the family within.

It is a warm May late afternoon. The garden, with the lawn and the shrubbery, the quince, and the mulberry tree, is bathed in western sun – the lilacs are out. The new green of the mulberry tree seen from the window is an arresting sight to everyone, like a new dress that is a perfect success and admired by all.

In the drawing-room, with its French window open, sits my mother, Mrs. Kestell, under a great piece of romantic tapestry representing a woodland scene, making tea for Mr. Oscar Browning, who is calling, and for Mr. Shorthouse, the author of *John Inglesant*, who is staying in the house. Her sister has ceased her Brahms sonata, closed the piano, and joined them.

Mr. Shorthouse gains much the most attention from my mother. Absorbed in metaphysical speculations, she is like a swift fish rising out of a river of doubt to catch small flies of certainty.

But Mr. Shorthouse has a stammer, which seems to throw him into a fit whenever he speaks.

In the quiet, comfortable study, with his white hair and a look of being half a medieval saint and half a country squire, my father sits correcting Latin verses at a great writing-table, while little boys knock at his door and come in, bringing him their books. There is a murmur of 'Yes, sir,' 'No, sir,' 'Well, you see, sir,' 'I don't know, sir,' 'Simply can't, sir,' 'Simply stuck, sir,' 'I don't know how to get on, sir.' He has a detached, imaginative grasp of all their characters, and looks up kindly over his eyeglasses at

19

them; and says something always kind, but often too clever for them; some of them see what he means when they have left the room and thought it over; others give it up.

Upstairs in her room Teresa, aged eighteen, is studying Greek for Mr. William Cory. She passionately enjoys the sights and sounds of the garden from her window, and draws a bee crawling into a columbine.

Susan, aged seventeen, is in the shrubbery. That afternoon in the garden she had stood for a moment under a hawthorn tree, and some petals of the blossom had fallen on to her hair and shoulders. Mother, strolling with Mr. Shorthouse, had exclaimed: 'O, stay, darling – under the hawthorn – how beautiful!' Susan had combated the self-conscious moment with an embarrassed smile and an elf-like rush out of sight into the little wood.

In the schoolroom tea is over, and Adela and Roderick are playing Diabelli duets together; two deathly pale children with any amount of vitality in their eyes. They wear the expression of two tight-rope walkers balancing themselves on ropes, for the effort of keeping time, reading notes, and managing their hands is great. Their concentration soon breaks down. They end in a wild noisy strumming, and then rush out into the garden to look for the strayed tortoise, to the relief of an elder brother, Henry, who is quietly reading *Redgauntlet* in a rocking-chair.

Upstairs in the nursery Evelina and I are on the floor, playing on the Kidderminster carpet. She is four; I am seven. She is making a garden with dandelions and cow parsley. She is fond of bringing in bunches of wayside weeds from our walks. I am simply lying there, chaunting idly and looking at things upside down. Eva, our nurse, doesn't approve; lifts me up off the floor and tells me to tidy the dolls' house. I start on this listlessly, for there is the usual old worry to face of the wrong proportions of everything inside the dolls' house that gives me an uneasy feeling of helplessness; the heavy gold tea-set goes over at a touch, and sends all the chairs falling about, and knocks down the dolls – and there are other difficulties.

But my eldest brother, Antony, aged sixteen, comes into the room. He suggests that the skeleton in the dolls' house cupboard is that the only male doll (known as the Baron) is a drunkard. There are scenes; it is natural that there should be furniture crashes. I remember learning the words 'Delirium tremens' at that moment, and being rather disturbed. The game does not attract me; the dolls' house is still out of favour. The presence of my favourite brother, however, is enormously cheering when we turn towards the table and Eva gives him tea. He has been fishing in the river and is late. He had decided against the schoolroom and the Diabelli duet players; drawing-room embarrassments he has avoided. His excuse once on being asked by my mother why he had abruptly disappeared after shaking hands with a visitor had been: 'Oh, I saw that he was a genius and hated me for not being one.' He is given up to country pursuits, and hardly ever indoors; but whenever he comes up to the nursery he is always very, very kind to me. My conversation becomes positively brilliant, thanks to his sympathy and flattering equality – he listens to what one says, and I seem to be quite grown up. He tells me now that the Mr. Shorthouse in the drawing-room below is a Birmingham vitriol manufacturer, and I add 'vitriol,' besides 'delirium tremens,' to my vocabulary.

CHAPTER TWO

But now it is time to go down to the drawing-room. We are seized on by Eva, and held swiftly and fiercely under sponge and comb. Coral necklaces are clasped round our necks, and sashes are tied on; and, once ready, we go downstairs with a festive sense of expectancy. I get to the bottom of the stairs first, and sit there waiting, for Evelina has to drop one foot deliberately down on to each stair, stop, and bring the other foot down cautiously after it; she takes her time.

Mr. Browning has left; Mr. Shorthouse is still in the drawing-room, but we are able to have a good read of Grimm with my mother and some jolly singing; but then, alas! *hymns!* The vitriol manufacturer has asked for 'We are but little children weak.' We stare at him, transfixed by the contortions of his stammer, and then reluctantly comply. By the time we have had two or three hymns I am reduced to a state of miserable depression. It always happens if we have hymns. We go to bed and Eva is out, there is only the comfortless nursery maid there; it is dusk; the gloom grows more and more as we undress. I creep into my bed, feeling utterly forlorn, and almost at once begin to be frightened.

Presently my mother comes to my bedside and I wail reproachfully, 'Oh, why did we have "We are but little children weak"?' but already by her presence – a little out of breath, in her comfortable velvet dress – she has soothed me. She strokes my chin with a deliciously soft hand over and over again. She stays with us till we drop off to sleep peacefully.

That particular day happened to end with a calm night. As a general rule after dark the nursery floor became crowded with wolves, and the knives of murderers and robbers gleamed from under the bed valances; the mad dog with foaming mouth galloped up the stairs and along the passages over and over again, only just missing our door in its hurtling rush; the ghost-woman, in a flannel petticoat with a lighted candle, slowly came round the door into the room and padded about. I could hear her – if I looked round I should see her. Even by daylight bad things happened. Eva, our nurse, for instance, once had her soul stolen away by dwarfs. Although she spoke and seemed almost the same, her soul had gone away. As she swept the room, as she poured out the tea, I knew she was only a carcass, a stock. I would watch her, pale with the strain of my secret, which I could share with no one.

Besides the concealing of night fears there was the hiding of humiliations to be managed. When my brother Roderick, at our breakfast table before a start on a journey to Devonshire, said, 'Look at little Mary, too excited to eat,' how I hoped that a wide agreeable smile would conceal my pang of humiliation! Fears, humiliations, and depressions were subtle, grim, secret; above all, these emotions were adult in their strength. I feel unchanged, and at this moment I see myself like an old sea that has been coming in and going out, coming in and going out on tides, for a very long time, with an unceasing murmur.

But apart from fears, humiliations, and depressions, I now know I was very happy; my time was spent flitting about a house full of very kind, very occupied people, and in dreaming and playing in a garden. I can remember one morning sitting up at the nursery breakfast table, holding a porridge bowl up to my lips and feeling the thick, rough stuff flowing slowly down my throat, and looking out over the rim of the bowl at our autumn garden and seeing that it was pure gold and superbly beautiful. Evelina and I used to roam about our house, opening doors and entering on dramas and peep-shows. You came into the schoolroom and you heard a scolding; then ran out, shutting in the sound of the stiff, chilblainy scales and the noisy tick of the metronome, to wander on to the study door. The handle was turned with difficulty; once inside the room there was my father and everything to do with him that concerned oneself. You felt the peculiar and pleasant electric shock of his prickly shaven chin against your face; and felt the delicious fresh smell of his very clean soap; there was his red sealing-wax and his ink; and you went out of the room with a picture he had drawn of an eagle carrying off a baby.

A great deal of music was played in the house. You would often find the drawing-room full of instruments and fluttering music and a conductor waving a wand; once a large lady stood up and sang marvellous songs about rushing streams and a wandering miller. There were visitors who were interesting to watch and who were very, very kind, and out of whose trunks came rustling tissue paper and caskets of jewels.

My mother had cabinets with drawers to examine, and she had boxes of jewels, too; and she made no fuss when Evelina, while playing, flung a diamond and ruby ring into her fire and all the gold was found to be melted away. She was very absent-minded with us. We would be dancing with exquisite enjoyment, bounding and flying about to her Weber strains or her Schumann waltz; and suddenly she would forget us and muse for a long time in silence at the piano; or she would begin telling us a most interesting story, and then she would stop and stroke our chins and look through us with a far-away look in a long pause, and one said in vain: '*Mother! Mother!* Oh, *do* go on.' She seemed too far away to hear. At last Evelina discovered that, if you said 'Mrs. Kestell!' in a very severe tone, she could be recalled, and with a smile she would at last go on.

Besides listening to her stories and reading and music, when we were little, we used to bury our noses in her bowls of roses and take great draughts of freshness from them, as she did, following her, and breathing it in, like her; and she would shut her eyes and take great draughts from the fragrance of a peach, and then we would shut our eyes and take great draughts too. It is difficult to give any idea of my mother's delightful but over-intense and eccentric personality. As her daughter I find her an elusive subject.

Ah! But those romantic, sheltered, Ruskinian days of my childhood were good! Our flowers, our Devonshire streams and valleys; our autumn garden with its

26

rustling leaves! I seemed to live then by rushing water – my feet were always on moss. And the poets told me God had made all on purpose for delight.

And you must know, no poet could then keep silent about nature. They felt mystery and majesty all round them and they seemed to make up a great choir or symphony about the spring and the sun and the earth and the water and the air on and on.

Some time ago I was sitting in the garden at Farringford, which now belonged to Tennyson's son, Hallam, but where the rooks were *still* 'crying and calling,' and reiterating, 'Maud! Maud! Maud!' and through the lane at the end of the garden came bouncing and bumping a yellow and red motor-van. A cry at the desecration came from the old gentleman who had led me there. He has died since. He lived on the island, surrounded with Mrs. Cameron's photographs, illustrations by Dicky Doyle, Fred Walker's water-colours, and Moxon's editions of the poets. He was then of dead yesterdays. He had ceased already to be expressive.

For now no poet would dare leave London at all for fear of the inspiration of a garden or a rill. They sit at home and do mathematics; and red and yellow vans are their delight. If a poet does stray into the country for inspiration, it shows a marked failure of vitality; and he must not feel the light and shade among the summer leaves, or 'the flying gold of the ruined woodland'; his poem will be of the mass of yellow flies seething up from the hot brown cow-dung; the pool where a trout is leaping may take his fancy, but in his poem a stark and pregnant cat must float upon its surface. Birds are now unfashionable in poetry. The lark that sang at Heaven's Gate, or ascended 'like a cloud of fire,' is utterly tabooed. Woollen birds worked in bright cross-stitch now have all the success.

The painters, too, show temper with the past. Natural flowers seem insipid in shape. Patterns of different coloured sands are more interesting; a little house-breaker's rubble, some scaffolding, a butcher's shop, and they have their landscape.

And prose? 'First of all, it has the great merit of meaning absolutely nothing!' says a young man describing the new book that was giving him entire satisfaction.

For a long time now the sound of crashing and smashing of glass has been in my ears.

It is the strong, rose-coloured glass of the ninteenth century conservatories cracking up. Now the wrecking is over. There is a great mess everywhere about, and something perhaps of the early morning misgiving after the spree. The detached biographess, hurrying out to view the damage, does so without betraying emotion; and yet, as she turns away, the Young with their hammers catch her murmuring: 'Stones for bread! Stones for bread!' and wonder what she is driving at.

CHAPTER THREE

When I was twelve years old my father was made Vice-Provost of Eton, and we moved into the Cloisters, which became our home until he died. The windows of our stately Tudor house looked over the Fellows' garden upon the Thames on one side, and on the other upon a meadow, through which a rapid brook flowed under willows to join the river; and in the distance, above higher trees, rose the towers and battlements of Windsor Castle. Adela, Evelina, and I had attics and a tower of our own, overlooking all this; and on close summer nights, when sleep was slow in coming and we heard the college clock strike every quarter above our heads, one or other of us would be constantly out of bed, padding from window to window, to look out at the river in the moonlight; at the poplar tree that was scarcely stirring, at the grey Castle with its few twinkling lights, and at the brook gleaming behind the willows. The husky cough of one of the shabby old sheep in the meadow down below would suddenly break the romantic spell for me; after one last draught of all this loveliness I would get back into bed.

In the winter the great fires still roared and crackled up the chimneys of every room, as they had done in our old house; but we had become poorer. My father's attacks of financial agitation, needless to say, were severer than ever. At such times it seemed to him, now that he was only a Fellow of the College, that we were living, not even in a garret of our own, but in the very workhouse itself. Financial family conferences were frequent, in which we younger children took part, simply because we were interested and were not driven away. In the panelled dining-room with its long windows, looking out on the Fellows Garden, and on the river beyond, an enormous account-book, together with a great pile of bills, would be flung upon the round table, and attempts at cutting down expenses would then begin.

This account-book was known as 'Le Grand Livre.' It was kept on a cryptic system devised by my father and mother in collaboration, and rigidly adhered to in spite of the fact that no one, not even they themselves, could work the system of analysis devised. The family account-book may seem a trivial matter to mention, but 'Le Grand Livre' played so large a part in my life before marriage that it must be brought into the picture. Yes, 'Le Grand Livre' must be mentioned; also the family portraits which looked down upon us seated round it, like detached, well-dressed people in the boxes at a realistic drama of everyday life. The Kneller in her green dress, the Beechey in rose brocade, with smiling expressions and gentle eyes, seemed perpetually interested in us, even when we were eating rice pudding. I liked to imagine that when no one was in the room they talked us up and down with 'Mr. Bathurst,' a gentleman of Charles II's reign, who always seemed particularly amused by us; I used even to fancy sometimes, while we were there, that their lips moved a

PORTRAIT OF THE VICE PROVOST OF ETON
(1893-1915) READING IN THE COLLEGE LIBRARY

little. There were also over each of the two dining-room doors trios of little, insignificant eighteenth-century people, like little pigs in evening dress, but they were not alive enough to come into my game.

At these conferences, my father, at other times vague and generous, would put on a rapid, practical manner, and holding up 'Le Grand Livre' some distance from his gold eyeglasses, he would note such minute matters as, for instance, that we had had forty Camembert cheeses in ten weeks: that must cease. My mother would then say this was perfectly absurd, that he understood nothing; that when, for instance, the Russian Ambassador had come to luncheon un-expectedly the day before, the Camembert had most economically saved the situation. She would then advance a whole string of unanswerable arguments in favour of Camembert.

'Well, then, *wine*?' The wine for dinner parties was a great expense.

'Yes, but you know how deadly dull the Bishop of Camelot's dinner parties are,' she replied; 'and it is chiefly because they have only very weak claret for the exhausted guests.'

My mother then would suggest that all animals and birds should be instantly put down: dogs ate bones, cats drank milk, birds cracked hemp. 'Now the parrot really *is* an expense,' I remember her saying; and drawing 'Le Grand Livre' to herself she read out, 'June—bird-seed, corn, sand. July—corn. August—hemp, corn.'

My father, who, she knew perfectly well, par-ticularly liked the parrot, turned impatiently from her irony, to leading the attack once more himself. And so

31

they would go on, detail after detail proving indispensable.

We all laughed at the absurd things that were said, and there was a great deal of argument. However, it must be granted that after one of 'Le Grand Livre,' conferences extreme general efforts at economy would be made. We should have hardly anything to eat for several weeks – and visitors were treated in the same way. Then suddenly a telegram from some delightful friend would come in, or, let us say, from Mr. Sven Hedin, wishing to see the College Library; or from some distinguished French *savant* who had taken a fancy to my father; or it might simply be a lovely spring day, giving my mother a sense of festivity – when chickens and salmon would be ordered, and lobster mayonnaise set in again, not to go out until the next financial crisis. Some of our friends noted these extremes, and used to ask one another, 'Was it fast or feast at the Cloisters when you were last there?'

Evelina and I missed our old garden with the mulberry tree and shrubbery when we moved into the Cloisters. We were awed by the Fellows' garden, where we offended gardeners and felt no freedom in our games; but the long gallery that ran round the Cloisters, the great studded doors labelled in brass, 'Bursar,' 'Provost,' 'Headmaster,' conduced to exciting flights when we played hide and seek.

My eldest sister, Teresa, who had a genius for teaching, had always given us children lessons up till now. She gave us an idea of the feudal system; she made the Wars of the Roses and the Hundred Years' War, with their character parts, quite exciting. We worked hard, but she taught us like a sister and not like a professional, and there was often a nice long pause in the lesson while she went upstairs to my father's study to probe, say, to the bottom of the character of Becket before telling us about the quarrel with Henry. But Teresa had now sailed for India to visit our relations. We belonged to one of those now old-fashioned families with uncles and cousins meting out justice in India, who spent their lives in carefully weighing in the scales Queen Victoria against millions of natives. The Lawrence tradition still survived; Mr. Keir Hardie had not yet visited a few places in India. A mass of traditional prejudice, I still believe firmly that the English rule in India has been a most marvellous feat. I belong, in fact, to the old 'Curry and Rice' school and I am utterly insulted at hearing that fine volume of history closed with an ungrateful bang.

Now that my sister was away, the town schoolmaster came every evening and taught us arithmetic and writing. He had no control over Evelina, who used to get up in the middle of his lessons and arrange the room for a steeplechase; and, whenever bored with sums, she leapt over the sofa and chairs she had arranged, round and round the room, calling out that she must take exercise, and that he could quite well correct the sums without her help. He submitted. While he sat meekly correcting and she continued flying over her obstacles, she would ask him questions. 'Do you like novels, Mr. Brown? Do you like Jane Austen's novels?' 'Well, Evelina,' I remember the poor man replying, as she cleared a chair or the Chesterfield, 'if Miss Austen's novels were re-edited

33

and half the matter cut out they *might* be readable.'

Evelina's spirits were high, and she was up to anything. I had bursts of wild spirits, too, but on the whole I was a quiet, contemplative child. I was very silent. I would say to Evelina, 'Father wants us to go for a long walk. Now, don't imagine I am going to speak a single world the whole time, because I am not.' And she would very easily and obligingly entertain the Vice-Provost, leaving me free to be as morose as I liked, as we took our way upon the Eton Street, meeting boys and masters; up the Windsor Hill under the Curfew Tower, meeting canons, aldermen, choirmen, guardsmen, and county-lady shoppers, and so, on and on, to Windsor Great Park, where perhaps in the late damp afternoon we would meet old Queen Victoria, driving home to tea behind her white horses and her outrider.

Now my mother, having come in one day upon the steeplechasing lessons, decided that really something must be done – anyhow for little Mary's better education. Unfortunately for me, she drove off next day for 'Marsh,' on the outskirts of Windsor, where a community of Sisters of Mercy ran a young ladies' college, a high school, an orphanage and a penitentiary. It was the bell of the young ladies' college she rang.

The Sisters of Mercy in their grace, with their long black robes, fresh white caps under their flowing veils and their silver crosses, seemed to her angelic. The long, white dormitories, the bees-waxed floors, the incense-laden chapel, gave her a sense of that disciplined order and calm she herself longed for, and would love to have implanted to a daughter. But oh, mother! you did not inquire about the fellow-pupils, about the food, the hours of work, the walks two and two in a 'crocodile.' There and then she sealed my fate. I was to be incarcerated in this High Church stronghold as speedily as possible.

For some twenty-four hours after my arrival I was sustained by curiosity; then no prisoner in the Chateau d'If could have felt more hopeless and forlorn than I did on the second morning of awakening in the frosty dormitory. At six o'clock, a servant lit the gas jet with a loud pop. She then rang a dinner bell round about and all over us, as though she were sprinkling us with the sound. (She was, by the way, a reformed penitent, and she had a wooden arm with a hook to it, like Captain Cuttle.)

Each morning I gulped and tasted my salt tears as her outrageous bell died away down the farther dormitories. Then fear pulled me together and braced my cold fingers for struggling with my buttons, tapes, and tangles; feeling sleepy and forlorn, I rushed down with the belated; and from that moment, all day, I was uttering the White Rabbit's cry, 'I shall be late, I shall be late.' Life became nothing but an unquestioning effort not to be left behind, and not to be too conspicuously incompetent.

I felt hopelessly out of it among the hundred girls, into whose bewildering giggling, chattering and scrambling I had suddenly been plunged. I did not think I should ever be anything but silent and depressed, so I concluded I should always be out of it. Everyone said, 'Why on earth did you come for the Lent Term? It's the worst of all; even beastlier food than in other terms, and everything's horrible.' As for the food, I will only mention here one dish which we called 'skilly.' This concoction was said to be a recipe from the workhouse. It was simply paste; served up in a great white pool for a hundred people, it was a very nauseating dish.

When the refectory meal was over on that first day, I was told we were all to assemble for the walk in the school courtyard; it was bounded on three sides by the ecclesiastical-school architecture, and on the fourth by the church. Thither I went, and loitered forlornly in the cold.

A chaplain in a biretta and a long black cassock flapped across it, and all the white pigeons strutting there rose up above his head as he passed on into the church. Other girls were now gathering in twos and threes for the walk; and very soon I was sandwiched between the flowing hair of the girl in front of me and the toes and nose of the girl behind, as the long 'crocodile' swung out of the courtyard and on into the suburbs, slums and dust-heaps into which the town of 'Marsh' degenerates. And at that very moment I knew Evelina at home would be skating on the frozen floods on the meads! She had written that she could even do the outside edge, and now she would be flying about over the ice in her little seal-skin jacket, as free as air, in the fields by the river under the Castle. Here at 'Marsh' was I walking with a perfect muff! For the new girls had no choice of a companion; they were engaged for the walks by girls who could not succeed in getting partners among their contemporaries. Mine had an old face and silly ringlets; her name was Mabel Parsley.

I gathered from her that the 'crocodile' rarely went

into fields or open country. We stuck to the roads on the outskirts of 'Marsh,' where the most bedraggled of that town always seemed the only passers-by: low-looking tramps trudging with sacks to the dust-heaps, or sad women wheeling perambulators full of washing or firewood, and coming along towards the gate we were reaching.

'That's the House of Pity we are passing now,' my partner said, as we turned up a lane and passed a building shut off from the road by a high wall and a solid wooden gate with a great knocker.

'What's that?' I asked.

'Oh, where the penitents are,' she said mysteriously.

'What are they?'

'Oh, bad women,' said Mabel Parsley. 'They do laundry work and are trained there.'

'Oh,' I said.

I had never heard of a harlot, so I supposed they had stolen things, or perhaps slaughtered people in tempers. Some penitents, in white caps, were at the moment carrying their washing baskets across the road, accompanied by a Sister of Mercy. I thought that they seemed to be thoroughly making up now for everything they might have done.

Meeting them was the best event on the walk. We 'broke rank' for a little; then the 'crocodile' pieced together its vertebræ again, and we filed home to sit at our desks for more lessons.

My misery increased and increased as I sat there at my desk, facing the crucifix on the schoolroom wall.

I admired the racked figure of Jesus with the dramatically pierced forehead, feet, and hands; and

37

with a kind of exquisite pang of dramatic sympathy, I felt the nails drive into my own palms and the thorns into my own forehead. My home-sickness had now become a chronic pain akin to physical sickness. I saw that I should be entirely shut off from my home life, with all its interests so near my heart, and shut in with the beringed and bangled, sweet-eating, 'genteel' herd, amongst whom I had suddenly been dropped.

Now, as the afternoon wore on, we were given a poetry lesson by one of the Sisters. I was tired out, and I could not help crying. I wept quietly and hoped I would not be seen, but one of the girls in the class noticed my plight, and as she stared at me in indifference, she seemed to me like some little evil goblin in the gloom. When my turn came to say my verse of the eternal 'Schooner Hesperus,' no voice came. I made a desperate effort to speak, but my throat was stiff with tears. Seeing my distress, Sister Anna Alexandra left her great desk and led me by the hand out of the room. She was the severest of the Sisters; a masculine type, thick-set with bushy eyebrows. I was far too frightened of her for her to be any comfort to me as she took me up the staircase, on through the dormitories, down the icy aisles of white beds, in silence; the starch of her white cap crackling under her black veil, as she marched forward in her draperies in a business-like manner with a manly tread.

We turned into the infirmary. Here there was a bright fire, and the beds were red. Anna Alexandra delivered me swiftly over to Sister Mary Elizabeth and turned and tramped away, back to the 'Schooner Hesperus.' The latter Sister rose from her seat, tall,

38

graceful and perfectly kind. She clasped my hand, with its miserable little ball of damp handkerchief, in her motherly grasp; she stirred the fire and gave me a cup of hot tea, with two convalescents who were sitting up in bed having theirs. Comforted by her genuine sweetness and goodness, I was soon convalescent, too, though my misery kept coming to the surface with sharp twinges.

After a little while Sister Mary Elizabeth said she thought I should like to go and see Father Eustace: she would take me to him and go and say her prayers in the church, where I was to join her afterwards. She swam gracefully forward with me, and I loved going with her, as once more I was taken along passages and down staircases. Finally we went up a short flight of stairs, at the top of which she knocked at a door; and then, smiling with a faint twinkle of merriment, she pushed me, ever so gently, with a little murmur of explanation, into a small parlour furnished with a crucifix, and a *prie-dieu*; and Father Eustace looking kindly towards me.

He was the chaplain I had seen crossing the courtyard in the afternoon. He sat at a table writing; and I sat before him, hoping my eyes were not still red, and wondering why I had had to come there.

Father Eustace wore merino mittens. He himself was a gentle mortal, and we looked dejectedly at each other across his writing-table. He seemed to be a kind of registrar, for he noted down in a book my birthplace and details of my religious education. Presently he handed me across the table a little devotional volume bound in purple, called *The Better Way*, and proceeded to go through some of the prayers with me. One beginning 'Hail, Mary, Mother of God!' he pencilled through, saying with a little sigh that the Bishop had settled this was not to be used by the girls at 'Marsh.'

We prayed together, and then he let me out; and I clattered away down his wooden stair. I liked getting a present, and I was delighted with *The Better Way*. I thought it would give me a fresh start. I would tell my sisters all about this visit to Father Eustace in his cell when I saw them again. *When* – ah! when?

It was evening now. I enjoyed the fresh rush of the free air in the courtyard as I ran across to the church to join Sister Mary Elizabeth at her devotions. The silent church was warm and smelt of incense; it was almost dark, save for the red glow of the ever-burning lamp. Mary Elizabeth, a black figure, knelt with other Sisters motionless in prayer. I went and knelt just behind her. The silence was heavenly; the church seemed very beautiful. I said my incoherent prayers that never had any style about them. I had been taught never to pray for material gifts, or for treats, but now I prayed: 'Oh, God, if it can come about, let it be that I shall be sent for to go home next Saturday. Oh, God, if it is only for a few hours, I beg and beseech you. Let it be that there will be a letter saying that I am to go home. Oh, God, you will for my sake! Oh, God, for Jesus' sake; oh, God, let it be. Oh, God, help me to get away, for Jesus' sake. Amen.'

Presently the church began to wake up for evensong. It began to blaze with light. A verger in a cassock lit candles on the altar with many ritualistic bowings to the East. Through the side door entered

40

the 'crocodile,' and Sister Mary Elizabeth gently sent me away from her to sit with it. The organ pealed. It was a Saint's Day; a choir trooped in in procession, and behind them a censer-swinger and candle-bearers. The Gregorian chants of the Psalms were very beautiful; we crossed ourselves at the end of the Creed.

I decided to be as High Church as it was possible to be, and genuflected low before the altar as we passed out.

CHAPTER FOUR

THE religion of 'Marsh' College now became my chief interest in life.

From a glass case in the hall (kept as a shop) I purchased two miniature ecclesiastical candlesticks; a crucifix, though coveted, was beyond my means, so I bought instead a sparkling mineral rock surmounted by a little marble cross. Equipped with this furniture, I made an altar in my cubicle, and every night and morning prayed long before it, *The Better Way* open before me. This book prescribed my day. As soon as I was awake and the clang of the penitent's bell had died away, I made an 'Ejaculation' to start the day. There was a whole chapter of 'Ejaculations' in *The Better Way*, and I got two into my day, for I made another at twelve, 'on hearing the clock strike.' My prayers were full of imagery. All day I was a pilgrim, 'watching soberly for roaring lions,' or pulling my stuck legs out of 'sloughs of Despond.'

Applying the searching questions set down by the author of *The Better Way*, my nightly self-examination discovered a mass of sin. There appeared to be no Commandment I had not broken, the seventh not excepted. For even under this heading *The Better Way* most ingeniously managed to bring in the young by making me ask 'Have I been curious about improper subjects – asking about them? Or told others?' and like all children about twelve years old, I was curious about what the compiler of the book considered to be improper subjects; that is to say about birth and marriage.

The fantastic modesty of Victorian parents no doubt produced inquisitive children, but in those days their curiosity was called 'morbid.' Modern parents see that their curiosity is 'natural'; and even the most delicate-minded teach their children the facts of life without feeling they have opened Pandora's box. Still, a child of the old *régime* as I was, it was surely time that I should gather somehow that children were not sent ready made as gifts into their mothers' arms. From Cécile, a friend, I learnt that children were born after the manner of calves and foals, and this was very interesting news; from Kathleen, another friend, I was about to learn more, but she grew frightened in the middle of imparting her valuable information. I can see Kathleen now with her flaming Scotch red hair, making her bed, with her bracelets jingling, flinging the blankets into place, thumping the pillows and teasing me as she withheld her superior knowledge.

Well, it was clear that according to *The Better Way* I had broken the seventh Commandment; but these things were so very interesting that this sin sat quite lightly on me. It was when I passed on to the eighth, 'Thou shalt not steal,' that my conscience was racked. I had put one day, in a moment of self-protection against daily scolding, for I was the dunce of the arithmetic class, a large confident *R* by the side of three sums which were decidedly wrong; I had wanted three Rs and I had put three Rs. Then I knew how all crime came to be done; I discovered, too, that after yielding to the moment's impulse one had to suffer the tortures of the damned. Unless I confessed to the Sister in charge of the class, I could never satisfy my conscience, yet this I could not do; for Sister Anna Alexandra, the severest woman I had ever known, would humiliate me. There was also a fatal contradiction in my troubled feelings. Besides not being able to confess because the crime was so grave, I also could not confess because it was so trivial. It was terribly important, yet foolish and unimportant. In vain I now steadily marked every sum, right or wrong, 'X' to atone for the fatal Rs; I could not get rid of the fear set up by the self-examination commanded in *The Better Way*. Night after night, tired and rather overstrained with a strenuous day, my conscience tormented me; and there seemed also to be perpetual allusions to me in Father Eustace's sermons and in what people said. I would be perfectly happy, when suddenly a twinge within would come, and a fog-yellow melancholy would settle upon me, and, lasting sometimes for hours, leave me exhausted. Finally, I could bear it no longer. As the coward at last takes his tooth to the dentist, so I unburdened myself. But I was wily, I *wrote* to Anna Alexandra; the unexpected happened, she was merciful. She answered me in a note and did not summon me to her side. 'Victory for God!' 'Triumph over the devil!' were much easier to bear in writing than while standing before her.

My private self-examinations and confessions threw me in on myself; confession-box and priest would have helped me more. It was a custom to pray a great deal in the warm and beautiful church, and thither I often repaired to pray alone, enjoying the space, the darkness, and the red glow of the ever-burning lamp among the images, in the blessed silence, away from monkey chatter.

Yet in the school itself, in spite of my conscience, the bitter cold, and my chilblains, I had by now quite recovered my spirits. I had now many friends. The speech of the Bandarlog was becoming my speech; and I was taken up by the fastest set in the school. Kathleen, Lucy, and Polly were noisy and daring; Muriel and Beryl were reckless and vain. They had a *culte*; we called him 'The Cherub.' In a scarlet cassock and a short white robe edged with lace, he bore a candle in the church processions, held up the Gospel for the priest to read, swung censers, and managed the little bell and properties during celebration. He was very dark and handsome, but, for my part, after one week of admiration, I had been completely disillusioned by seeing him out of his robes, eating a biscuit on a bicycle. Although the set were unshakable in their adoration, for some reason it amused them that I had been so sadly disillusioned, and they enjoyed being told he was 'a perfect horror'; it added to the interest of the whole matter. Whispered jokes about him were fun for a while, but suddenly – it was as if I had been too long in stale air – it seemed as if there were no charm, no delicacy anywhere.

'I want to get out of this set. I don't know what I'm to do to get out of it. What *am* I to do?' I groaned to Birdie, who was not in it, and whom I myself had now begun to admire. Birdie, who had the colouring and eyes of Hogarth's shrimp girl, was very pretty. She lived in St. John's Wood, and described the gay nights and squalid days of a home quite different from my own. She had no mother, and she and her brothers

45

and sisters depended on the yearly sale of her father's lush, accomplished Academy pictures.

In earlier days this R.A. had been a disciple of the Pre-Raphaelites, who had had for a time high hopes of him. Then Birdie had suffered privation. But now the paints oozed quickly from his tubes and the family went to school.

I can best sum Birdie up as a 'Steerforth'; she could get one to admire her when she was quite unadmirable. She never had the smallest trouble over anything; during the arithmetic class her cheek bulged with a sugared almond; during preparation she read *Vanity Fair* to herself every day and it escaped notice; she had a love-correspondence with a medical student at Bart's, and firmly licked up her envelopes, which, by the rules of our prison, she ought to have left open for inspection. She had 'only written to an old doctor friend of her father's,' she said, when at last Sister Mary Elizabeth swept ever so gently and kindly up to her to make a little deprecating inquiry as to why so strict a rule had been broken.

She and I, in a reckless moment one day, had given to all the deathly white busts in the drawing school pink chalk cheeks, and blue chalk centres to their eyes. It was I who bore the punishment alone; she never owned to any of the damage. When I bought an acting edition of *Blue Beard* and suggested getting up the play in secret, having fancied myself calling with extraordinary dramatic energy, 'Sister Anne, Sister Anne, what do you see?' she seized it from me, took the best part for herself, and said, '*You* must be the Sheikh of the Desert – it's a very good part.'

I shot Birdie dead with an arrow of hatred sent flying from the gloomy fortress of my detached perceptions, over and over again; but she held her sway. She was full of effrontery, but she had so much charm. She took the best and left the rest. She was not a lady, but they are rare everywhere; and they were very scarce here, except among those beautiful black veiled forms, dedicated to a narrow, fanatical, but heroic law, who floated among us, ministering to us.

Well, I began to avoid 'the set.' Alliance with Birdie, who was their enemy, made open rupture inevitable. Then as luck would have it, just as I had broken with them and wriggled like an eel away, to my horror and complete surprise the Cherub *culte* was discovered, putting me in the position of a deserter. Two of the set had corresponded with the Cherub for some time and he had responded, being very careful not to say which of them he loved the best. One of the letter-writers was observed by a Sister of Mercy flinging a note out of the window at the Cherub, imploring him to declare himself. The note was confiscated, and the Cherub himself had been caught by the Vicar smiling at his loves during celebration. It looked, unfortunately, as if I had known they were going to be found out, and had retreated in time. Some believed in me, others didn't; I had left the set simply because I hated it, but I was tongue-tied. I could not explain, and felt myself at best a prig. The two worst culprits were summoned to the vestry to be scolded by the Vicar, and brought before their hastily summoned parents, who were forced then and there to remove their daughters.

It was now Mi-Carême, and my mother had written that she was getting up a pageant of months, and 'did so want little Mary for the part of February.' It was noticed that I was looking very sick and tired and cold; it would do me good to get a few days' change, the ever-kind Mary Elizabeth said. So I was put into a fly and sent home.

My well-brushed hair (nowadays my hair would be described as 'bobbed,' but according to my romantic mother I wore it 'à la Jeanne d'Arc'), my brown velvet dress, donned suddenly in the middle of the school week, gave me a Sundayfied feeling. Though the fly had an everyday musty smell, though Peascod Street seen from its windows was full of everyday shoppers, though I was soon rolling softly through Eton, and saw boys in shorts kicking footballs before them, I still had this Sunday feeling strong upon me: even when I walked into the house and ran, most expectantly, upstairs to meet my family.

I opened the drawing-room door; the musical genius, the composer, was at the piano alone, rehearsing the overture. I shut the door quickly so as not to disturb him, having taken in at a glance the bright fire, the river and castle through the windows, the azaleas, the strong-scented jonquils in pots, the Morris chairs. I opened the dining-room door; my mother's ardent greeting met me at once, making me a little limp and seemingly ungrateful and cold, as was my unfortunate way. The room was filled with beautiful young women metamorphosing themselves into months of the year; there were young slips for the early months, voluptuous girls for the hotter summer months, intense and spiritual creatures for those of the dying year. August was making a poppy wreath, June was engaged with roses; all were at work on properties – strawberries, blue and yellow irises, holly and ivy and corn. Evelina was having a rehearsal of her part alone, and could only wave to me from a corner.

'Mary, darling, you must *at once* start on your February part,' said my mother, kissing me enthusiastically again. 'Put on your dress and begin.' It was too much for me; the feeling of strangeness had not gone; I turned away suddenly, and went up the staircase alone. There in the solitude of my mother's bedroom I sat on a chair, terrified at the prospect of acting, and most miserable of all to find myself actually in tears at the prospect. But she, of course, had instantly understood; hurrying breathless after me, she consoled and encouraged me. One always stopped crying to hear what she was saying; it was so very remarkable, though, of course, as it was only one's mother's praise, the praise itself was nothing. Then she poured out a glass of sal volatile, so stiff that it went at once to my head, and I was able to rush downstairs and take the part of February with some success straight away. In a pale-green floating frock with long white petals, a little breathless after such a rapid *volte-face* from dejection, I ran on to the stage carrying a pot of snowdrops, and gave January (Evelina), a little girl in a brown hood, a hearty kiss, saying,

Sister, joy to you. I've brought some snowdrops.
Only just a few!
But quite enough to prove the world awake;

49

and so on and so on till March, a great breezy girl, in her turn, came blustering on.

The whole performance was a Pre-Raphaelite, intense affair. With its pale, half-toned colours, its naturalistic flowers, its romantic music, it was all that is most out of fashion now; and, tossed up into a lumber room, 'The Pageant' will probably lie there for thirty more years at least – then down one day it will come again, sure enough. 'Deliciously nineteenth century!' someone will say, imagining the properties, the flowers, and pale dresses. 'How heavenly for them to have been so intense, so romantic, and so religious!' a second will exclaim, turning Christina Rossetti's pages. 'We *must* revive it,' all will cry. Thus a sophisticated renaissance comes about.

My few days at home, acting, laughing, and talking far into the night with January, April, and other months, were orgies of delight. Then I got meekly into the Black Maria which arrived to take me back to school. I say meekly, for the Kestells were educated in the Casabianca tradition; one stayed where one was put. 'Where the goat is tied, there she must browse,' was our proverb; and rebellion, unfortunately for me at that moment, had not yet become the hallmark of the promising young.

The provincial horse-bus has, of course, died out; but in those days, if you ordered that it should be done, a horse was harnessed to a vast conveyance, and a neat man in livery and gloves rattled away to any distant part of the town. The windows of this 'bus rattled with a stinging, shattering, deafening noise. If you were inside with a friend of your own age you could shout against the noise and have fun and laugh over it; but alone even with Janet our dearly beloved maid in the dark, I seemed accompanied by a hundred yelling devils. At last I alighted. The page-boy opened the wicket-gate, and once more, my home life thrust quite out of sight, I plunged obediently into the life of the Bandarlog.

CHAPTER FIVE

IT continued bitter cold all that Lent. Our colds in the head were terrific; one girl had pneumonia in a room adjoining our dormitory, and the sound of her ravings is vivid to me to this day. Father Eustace padded down through the frost-bound passages one night, accompanied by black-veiled forms, to take her the last sacrament. But she recovered from her illness; she survived.

Then there was Barbara G's St. Vitus's dance, too. She was pretty, lifeless, well dressed, and unhappy. Feeling ill and weak, she was slack at her lessons, her brain was anæmic, and she looked vacant. Sister Anna Alexandra said that she was lazy, and that she did not exert her will. She clapped a dunce's cap upon her head. Barbara, after appearing two days thus coifed, suddenly lost control over her limbs. She danced and shuddered involuntarily. We scattered in consternation away from her in all directions, and she was removed from our midst. We could not tell if poor Barbara's spasmodic capers reproached Alexandra. We only hoped so.

And now the great drama of Holy Week had begun; and the altar and images were shrouded in black. Father Eustace and the curates, by this time much exhausted with Lenten fast, took more and more services; processions of black-veiled forms threaded even more and more often through our midst to the church for prayer and office; the church was alive with devotion, and was lived in by day and night.

Never shall I forget the absorption of the fine religious mood into which the school now merged itself.

From the day before Good Friday until Easter Eve total silence reigned throughout the building. Not a word was spoken in the refectory. We ate in silence, though we were allowed to read our books. We lived almost all day in the church. The loneliness and agony of Jesus in the garden, on the Mount of Olives, were real to us; it was all happening at that actual moment. We were present.

At last came the great Three-hours' service during the Crucifixion; and the seven words from the Cross; the bell tolled twice; there was a long hush. It was finished. The emotion had been tremendous.

The dignity of that dramatic Lent was inspired by ritual and worship. The inspiration came from Rome. The position of the very extreme High Church Party in the Church of England seems to me sadly isolated; I long to see them all under the wing of the Pope.

Easter Day found us in church again with the coming of morning. The black wrappings had been removed, and everything was white and gold, and festive.

After the celebration we trooped into the refectory to find row upon row of eggs in egg-cups, like lines of tiny bald men on guard for the festival. When we were seated, a door at the farther end opened and the old, old Sister Superior, who very rarely appeared before us, stood there like an apparition, and said in a faint voice, 'A happy Easter, my children.' 'Oh yes, the Resurrection!' I exclaimed under my breath, as we rose respectfully with a clatter, then clattered down again to our eggs. Her look, like some picture of one risen from the tomb, had suggested the idea, but I did not quite know what I had meant. I wondered a moment after. I think now it meant that my fine religious mood was over. We were but children, and we had had enough; I could stand no more; I wanted Easter to be gay and secular.

And now in a very few days our trunks were bumped down from the box-room, and we drove joyfully away. I took the long journey to Devonshire, to join my family, all by myself. When the train dashed into Barum Station it suddenly seemed as if the sun came gleaming out. After all, it was only Tom Huxtable, the coach driver, whose scarlet coat, silver-grey top-hat, and gaiters, were resplendent as he stood on the platform. My father liked trustworthy quiet Tom who knew us all and helped the constant family arrivals and departures.

He had brought a note to the train from my mother, and said he had orders that I was to sit by his side on the coach for the twenty-mile drive before me.

My mother was a great sender of notes, full of emphatic injunctions, often a little difficult to carry out. Evelina had complained of a message on one of our former arrivals with our nurse of the *infra dig.* caution 'to put one hand in the coachman's pocket and one hand on the rail of the coach.' But this time my solitary arrival had been quite worthy of a grown-up, and the note now did not spoil it. It contained no injunctions. It was full of interesting, if quite irrelevant, matter; the death of Lord Tennyson's shepherd, for

54

instance; the poet Clough was quoted; the word 'fantastic' was used and explained. 'Fantasy, Fantastic,' I vaguely conjugated as I clambered presently up the ladder on to the front seat. I wondered if Huxtable had read the note.

First we drove through lanes among orchards, then up and up to the airy moor. I was full of silent rapture up there on the coach behind the four horses, driving on and on for the long twenty miles to freedom; comfortably insignificant to the passengers, whose scraps of talk mingled with my day-dreaming. I climbed down the ladder and walked up the hills with the other passengers when the burden had to be lightened for the horses, but being in Huxtable's charge I was not allowed inside the 'Fox and Goose' Inn when we stopped half-way. I was fed and watered outside with his horses; pails and nosebags for the horses; tea and bread and butter handed up to me.

Then at last Tom charioted his four steeds down the last steep hill at a reckless gallop, and Helios-like swept up on the other side as on a cloud or a billow, landing them, with a last long stretch of their legs, in the village.

And yet, for all this gaiety, a fell Fate, unseen of human eye, hovered above this coachman's head the while. Six months later he lay dead in the 'Fox and Goose' with a bullet through his head. Beneath his handsome suavity he bore the burden of some intricate depression. He chose death and shot himself. I do not know the cause. The West Country is emotional; such tragedies are not uncommon among its people. Oblivious, at that moment of arrival, however, of the precariousness of human happiness, I climbed down off the coach and said good-bye to him, thanking him for looking after me. Adela and Evelina had come to meet me, and we all three ran laughing away down the steep lane and out to our house above the sea; wheeling and screaming with pleasure like the gulls below us in the evening sunlight.

There is quite a stir and bustle in the house on my arrival; I am kissed and made a great deal of. I go all over the house and look out of every window. Then after a while I just fit comfortably down into my place in the family again.

At dusk we come into the drawing-room and the lamps are brought in. Antony, who has been out hunting, begins cards with Adela, Evelina, and me; Mr. Kestell, at the piano in a far corner of the room, is playing and singing Mozart's 'Così fan tutte' gently to himself, but no one is paying any attention; everyone is talking out loud; Mrs. Kestell, over by the fire, has Newman's *Apologia* on her lap; Henry and Roderick, who have been trout fishing, have now also settled down by the fire; they are a little cold to her when she pleads for the Cardinal.

'Certainly he is very narrow over Adam and Eve and the Fall,' she concedes.

'It wasn't a fall at all. It was an advance!' says Roderick severely, looking up from his holiday task.

'And Carlyle says he had no more brains than a rabbit,' says Henry, looking up from *Mr. Sponge's Sporting Tour*.

Mrs. Kestell, among her family, often feels herself

to be a little like Alice among the unsympathetic animals of Wonderland.

The music ceases; Mr. Kestell comes over to the fire. He changes the subject, and begs Miss Mary Coleridge, our guest, who has volumes of Browning piled about her arm-chair, to read out some of the *Flight of the Duchess* or some other poem, before dinner.

'*Mine. Mine.* I was certainly first; it's mine,' comes from the card-players.

> I am a goddess of the Ambrosial Courts,
> And save by Here, Queen of Pride, surpassed
> By none whose temples whiten this the world.
> Through heaven I roll my lucid moon along;
> I shed in hell o'er my pale people, peace;
> On earth I, caring for the creatures, guard
> Each pregnant yellow wolf and fox-bitch sleek,
> And every feathered mother's callow brood,
> And all that love green haunts and loneliness.

Mary Coleridge reads, in a low intense voice, from *Artemis Prologizes*, till the cough of an old judge, who is paying his annual visit to us, breaks in. It is a geyser explosion, a thunderstorm, the collapse of a skylight, something quite unique in volume of crashing sound. The unintellectual side of the room is convulsed with a well stifled *fou-rire*.

More reading; then a loud gong.

Through the dining-room door the great tureen and pile of plates are seen.

'Let's have charades after dinner,' says Teresa as we file in. 'No, an opera – let's have an opera,' we cry.

And so the traditional family goes on. It is the

nineteenth century. All is safe. Such a calamity as the Great War is unthinkable. Queen Victoria has us in keeping. Released from my stern school, as I lie down in my bed, with the murmur of the sea in my ears, I am as happy as a little caterpillar on a fresh green leaf.

CHAPTER SIX

I w a s taken away from 'Marsh' after two more terms; from the skilly, the cold, and the squalor, and returned to the schoolroom at home. But I took with me the High Church fervour.

Adela was now nearly grown-up, and Evelina had her own friends with whom she went out for lessons; I was thirteen and Teresa had decided to teach me by myself. In the little brown-panelled schoolroom I sat preparing, alone; and the relief from my school life was very great. I liked my father's appearing at the door for a few minutes to talk to me, saying something interesting perhaps about Simon de Montfort or Joan of Arc (in our days children never seemed to get on to modern history). I liked, too, my mother's coming in and sending me on pleasant interruptive errands about the house or into the garden.

Perhaps it would be to remind the College Bursar to be sure and tell the gardener that there must be no yellow in the College bedding-out, of which she had seen a threatening in the pots he was mustering in his wheelbarrow in the distance; that as there were at least one hundred calceolarias already in the greenhouse, she could not stand any more. At school one never had such interruptions. There one never flew out into a garden to smell the lilac and the Indian currant, and to feel the summer warmth upon the lawn, or to have a chat in a potting-shed with a large bearded gardener who looked like Neptune. He tells me that his wife irons him with a hot iron every night for his rheumatism, and that he finds it comfortable.

But I hardly like to mention the gardener or even the garden; for both gardeners, who were kind of jesters to the families to which they were attached, and gardens were already beginning even then to be over-written.

The 'Capability-Browns' of the time were setting to work to sentimentalise and commercialise; grouping and massing, sending pink creepers and ramblers greedily rushing over pergolas. And ever since, things have gone from bad to worse. The place of the man who spits into his hands before thrusting into the earth a spade, has now been taken by a professor paid professorially for tending cushions of Aubretia in a 'crazy pavement,' and producing in a couple of seasons the 'Old World' garden, which has become the phrase of auctioneers. It is not to be wondered at that the young find these improvised 'Haunts of ancient peace' uninteresting; and it explains, perhaps, why they should have taken into favour by contrast 'The mandrakes, and toad-stools, and docks and darnels,' prickly and pulpy cactuses, Gauguin-like exciting poinsettias; and even the wax fruit and flowers of early Victorian days.

Then there were other interruptions to these leisurely studies. People it was a surprise to see would come into the schoolroom. Perhaps Maurice Baring, who was at this time an attaché at the Embassy in Paris, but a constant visitor at the Cloisters, would suddenly open the door, and either urge Evelina and me to be as naughty as possible, or, following

ETON COLLEGE, WITH FELLOW'S EYOT AND
THE WEIR STREAM IN THE FOREGROUND

what I was working at, sit down to lessons himself, and write a life of Simon de Montfort in another copybook; or if one happened to be doing German and Goethe, he might paint in a few minutes a dream-picture of Faust's last night on earth.

I was very lazy; my mind was constantly wandering. I see myself gazing out of the window over the top of *The Baron's War* propped up on the table, out beyond the stream and the willows, up at the grey castle, and wondering what is going on up there. Let us see it as it may have been.

The Royal Standard is flying from the Round Tower, for Queen Victoria is at Windsor. Let us pry in at the Castle, but do let us for once not see the Queen with her despatch-box, signing papers, with her Indian servant behind her – having been up since six. Let us more comfortably suppose she has a slight cold and has for once decided not to get up. So I see her leaning back on her pillows with her knitting and the *Times*.

The service in the Royal chapel is just over. Vergers with silver wands are closing the gates of the choir; and are barricading and shrouding everything they can. The prayer for her 'gracious Majesty Queen Victoria and all the Companions of the most honourable and noble Order of the Garter' has been intoned by a Canon; the blessing and the last Amen have been given; Dean, Canons, and Minor Canons disperse. The Dean takes his leisurely way through the Windsor Cloisters, passes under Anne Boleyn's chamber, and up into his library to his letters and work, to his *Church Times*, his ecclesiastical biography, his chair by his great fireplace. The Canons and Minor Canons

61

scatter through still older and more mouldering Cloisters, climbing winding staircases, to thick-walled chambers; the aristocratic old ladies, prayer-books in hand, disappear into Norman towers and Saxon towers, towers of Henry III and the Edwards. Those fine old 'Military Knights' with their cocked hats, who have sat in an imposing row through the service, every one of them looking like a field-marshal, have burrowed into their battlemented dwellings. Sir Walter Parratt, Master of the King's Music, and the most exquisite organist in England, has played out the shuffling congregation with some celestial Bach. Now he comes down from his loft. On his brisk walk to the railway station he makes several depressed residents perfectly happy for a few moments as he greets them, with his delight-ful bracing charm; he jumps into his train and plays chess all the way to the Royal College of Music.

It is a bright sunny morning. At the Castle gate-way the Guard is changing; bayonets gleam in the sunshine; the word of command echoes under the arch; a rattle of rifles follows. Then a little body of busbied Grenadiers comes on up the hill, marching all round about the Castle, dropping sentries and picking up sentries. You enter into the relief from ennui of the picked-up man swinging into step with the others, also into the mood of silence which en-velops the man dropped, as his comrades' marching footsteps die away. Surely, if he happens to be of a patient, receptive disposition, it must be pleasant being on sentry duty up at the Castle. For instance, out there – on the North Terrace 'bosomed high in tufted trees' – he can actually look down into rooks' nests!

However stiffly he must hold himself, he can watch the winding river, the boats like water-beetles upon it, and the lively town down below him; the carts and carriages, the hawkers, children, and dogs, coming down the hill under the Curfew tower. He can see into the crooked streets which run out to the river where the poor swarm, and the Italian organ-grinders and ice-cream men live. He can see, too, right out into the shire with its heavy elm trees; and there to the right, a little way across the meadows, he sees Eton College, its dark brick towers and battlements. If he had very good eyesight he might even see me, a speck, as, yawning and shutting up my book, I come to the window and lean out to enjoy the panorama which also contains him, keeping guard in scarlet among grey battlements.

CHAPTER SEVEN

THERE is a feudal and formal order about Windsor and Eton; set out together in the middle of the flat landscape, the two little towns have just something of the air of opposing white and red chessmen upon a board.

The white queen, knights, prelates and pawns of Windsor, flanked by the Castle towers, stand arrayed, and facing them are the powers and the pawns and the red battlements of Eton.

The picturesque feudalism of Windsor, however, might well seem to have quite died out, when its only representative was an ancient Queen with bonnet strings and funereal black kid gloves, who drove daily in a landau to visit a mausoleum in her park. Yet, often, as we sat late in the evening in the Cloisters drawing-room with windows open to the still night, there would be wafted across the river, clear and faint, the enchanting lilt of the 'Last Post', sounded on the bugle from the Castle garrison; and then Windsor belonged at once to Henry V, to Shakespeare, and to Herne the Hunter riding madly through the glades of the forest.

Sitting alone, sometimes, with my mother, at that moment, I noticed, she would shut her eyes, with a little intake of the breath, as though the distant music had lifted her suddenly out of the reverberating worries and dull exasperations of the past day, into romance; and the 'Last Post' would be an overture to a mood of reverie for both of us, as we sat there in silence, hearing now only the faint rush of the weir and the stir of the poplar tree.

But these were romantic moments. Shakespearean kings, Herne the Hunter, or the Chase, were hardly suggested to one, for instance, by the sleek deer that trotted about the Castle park. Haunches of venison were sent yearly by Queen Victoria as a gracious gift to the Fellows of the College; and now I see a picture of the white-capped College cook passing a haunch through the hatch which joined his pantry to our larder, and trying to reassure our own uninitiated cook, as she received it from his hands, that a curious gift of high mutton had not been sent from Windsor that it would be madness to roast for the Vice-Provost.

Evelina and I could not take any real part in the life of the school, though it pressed upon us on all sides with its running, kicking, batting, rowing, loafing boys. Life was accompanied by the thud of innumerable footballs during 'kick about' all the winter, the tap of bats during 'knock about' all the summer, the echoes of racquet courts, the rattle of the fives courts, the hoarse roar through the November mists at House matches, or the fierce, excitable shouting at 'Hoisting' after races on the river.

A great pile of dilapidated top hats outside a schoolroom, an open door emitting a voice sending out Latin words; then, presently, a scuffle and a pouring out of boys right upon one as one passed – that was all we knew of the school work.

Of course, the swarm of boys was taken as a matter of course by Adela, Evelina, and me; and yet,

65

F

instinctively, we went about looking for sanctuaries, preferring to seek shelter at those hours when they swarmed in their numbers. But if one chanced to attempt to get through the great quadrangle at the moment before 'Absence' was called, all was up, for in two seconds, one felt like a penguin when the beach has been invaded by a swarm of skua-gulls.

Amidst all the clamour of the boys, there was no-where for us to shout. When we had a modest game of hide and seek round about the Cloisters and passages, the cantankerous College butler told our maid that 'If the Miss Kestells made such a shindy in the gallery, they would have the Provost complaining – that's all!'

Adela and Evelina agreed with me that our Elizabethan house with the library, the cloisters, the gallery and the river, made a paradise of a home, but that a boys' public school was a hampering place for a girl to live in.

The few privileges we wrested from the school, such as swimming in the various pools, or fencing in the drill hall, were stealthily taken at odd hours.

However, though jealous of their privileges, we adored the boys. We were interested in them, though we shrugged our shoulders at the idea of having any direct communication of any real interest with them.

Evelina was always in love with one of the Eleven, and I teased her because she was pleased when her acquaintanceship with one particular swell involved the taking off of six hats of six swells walking abreast. But the adored one never knew of her feelings. She would appear to be reading a book under the trees in the playing-fields rather than watching his fielding and his batting. Pride took this form; and I, too, would not confess to having any preferences in this great male community.

'But you know you get as red as a turkey cock whenever we meet Dash Major,' Evelina one day most annoyingly exclaims.

'Yes, but will you understand it's only because he collided with me in the cloisters, rushing round the pump corner full tilt with his football. He ran straight into me and nearly knocked me down, and now, whenever we meet, we are both embarrassed, and I hate him for making me get red and wish him at Jericho.'

But it was only at Eton that I would not be susceptible.

With a brother of one of my friends I fell in love. He was at Wellington; a boy with a grave manner and a very individual charm. Every evening, on my visit to his country home, he took me out shooting rabbits and shared his gun with me as a matter of course.

Clambering over stone walls, strolling about the fields tinged with gold in the evening light, returning in the dusk to an old country house that had begun to twinkle with lights, in unselfconscious companionship and sympathy; that time seems to me now, on looking back, to have been perfect. Alas! he was killed at nineteen in one of our frontier wars. A flash and he was gone, like a star that drops suddenly from among the myriads on a summer night.

At the beginning of each term at Eton a list was made of those boys who should be invited to breakfast on Sundays. The list was very long, and few could be invited a second time in a term, so we could not get to know them well. Perhaps one had got over the preliminaries of communication and might be just getting on, when the chapel bell would go and they were off. We would follow them to the chapel for the eleven o'clock service. Though now broad church, I still liked ritual and would have much preferred to go to the service at 'Marsh'.

After the service I go out to the garden with my mother, and we pace down the path.

'It's too distracting a place, the chapel, mother,' I say, a little defiantly (I am annoyed that the Vice-Provost is so insistent on our attendance). 'We are cooped up in that pew like hens! Behind us, Mr. X says a part of the Creed with a firmness I can't understand, mother. He says "The Resurrection of the *Body*" with profound conviction. What can he mean?'

'Oh, he comes of a very Evangelical family. He is used, I suppose, from childhood, to saying it like that. As it happens I had a talk with him once about religion,' she continues, as we stroll along by the herbaceous border enjoying the sun, the scented pinks, the heavy, velvety bees. 'He himself would like to see the State governing the Church. If he *could* put a lion and a unicorn on the altar in the place of a cross, he would,' she says, smiling.

I would like to continue talking to my mother about Mr. X's curious opinions, but Evelina is seen at an upper window, and she suddenly begins practising on her little fiddle like a devil. Mrs. Kestell makes a sound as if her teeth were on edge.

'Go up and tell her to stop; she will disturb the College.'

So I rush up to the schoolroom and say:

'You're to stop at once; you'll disturb the College.' The formidable 'College' baulks all spontaneity.

Presently the gong sounds for the Sunday beef and Yorkshire pudding, and the family drops into chairs all round the table with abstracted expressions on their faces, brought away from their various occupations.

Roderick, who is at home from Cambridge, is writing an essay on Defoe, and so we talk about Robinson Crusoe, which suits Evelina and me.

Our friend Maurice Baring suddenly comes into the room from Paris. He produces from his bag what he calls 'Das Gepäck,' a scissors and paste anthology, to the making of which innumerable books have been extravagantly mutilated.

After luncheon we all go up into the gallery of College Hall to hear the Latin Grace sung, and all lean over and have a good look at the boys in their black gowns, seated at the tables below. The unique College Hall smell of beer and bread reaches our nostrils; so peculiar and ancient that it seems to come from crumbs never quite swept up since Queen Elizabeth's reign, and from beer served to Henry VI's scholars.

And now comes Sunday afternoon – hated by Evelina and me. We are not allowed to go on the river or even to play croquet. We go for a walk, and there are black coats and top hats to be seen everywhere against the green of the fields, and under chestnut trees and elms. On our return we sit in the garden with Collects to learn and Bible passages to study; but Evelina has also Poe's *Tales of Mystery and Imagination*, and I have *Pendennis*, and take half an hour with it before returning to my ecclesiastical studies. Besides the prayer book, I have Canon Gore's *Creed of a Christian*, for I am about to be confirmed, and, as usual, in a state of perplexity over metaphysical matters. The confirmation classes I go to weekly are dry and leave one cold. Fortunately, at home, one is left to oneself.

I do not talk to Evelina about my difficulties. I only tell her, now, that after the last class, I was taken by the clergyman into his study for a lesson by myself, and that it had been most uncomfortable, as he had suddenly asked me what my besetting sin was. I had replied 'Sloth!' 'One never uses such a word in real life; it was the churchy atmosphere that made me say "Sloth" instead of "laziness"!' says Mary.

'The fact is, you and I are both shy, and always things are happening that make us feel uncomfortable,' says Evelina, biting a daisy.

'Yes! What a bother it is!' says Mary with a sigh.

Evelina says that when she is confirmed, if she is asked this question she will not answer.

Presently we stroll across the lawn and up into the drawing-room, where we find our mother seated with a man who has come home on leave from India. He is in the same regiment as my eldest brother, Antony.

'The most sporting event of all Asia, Mrs. Kestell!' he is saying with loud emphasis. 'The Kadir Cup is the pig-sticking competition of *all* India, you know. Extraordinary that he did not tell you he had won it!' I am sent to rummage among Antony's latest letters, and we find that there has, in fact, been a modest account of this event, and of his wonderful mare, upon which he had won the cup; but Mrs. Kestell is apt to grasp the contents of her letters sometimes weeks after their arrival, for she has a nervous aversion to the post. Her opened letters are all tossed into a great china bowl on her writing-table, and are perused by us all at odd moment, so that she knows news will reach her eventually, and that we shall pester her into making replies to her letters in time.

Mrs. Kestell now becomes absorbed in the thought of her absent son. She gives close attention to all that her caller tells her for some time; but presently she begins to think about Antony himself, and looks through the sporting man abstractedly. 'Spear – frayed trouser – tusks – those appalling "nullahs" you know' (repetitions of his first narrative) reach her only in a dream; she is not listening to him. Teresa comes to the rescue and continues the conversation.

Several boys now enter, followed presently by Mr. Kestell, who brings in a Colonial bishop. He takes him to a sofa at the far end of the room for a chat. 'The larger the river, the bigger the fish are,' comes from the sporting man, who has now carried Teresa on from pig-sticking in India to fishing in Scotland. The next minute Adela and I, who have gone to a side table to cut up a melon with which to regale the bishop, hear our mother asking – we can hardly believe our ears – the Captain of the Boats if he is a 'Dry-Bob.' *

Adela and I exchange glances. The melon slips about as she cuts it, and the 'perforated' spoon in my hand showers the sugar over the cloth; we recover quickly from our hidden *fou-rire*.

* Boys at Eton who go in for cricket are called 'Dry-Bobs.' Boys who go in for aquatics are called 'Wet-Bobs.'

'No, a Wet-Bob,' is the modest reply of the Captain of the Boats. Except for these mistakes, Mrs. Kestell does, in fact, get on quite well with boys who are athletic; she loves boys, and appreciates their grace in all directions. It is not only the delightfully conversational intellectual boys who get on with her. She appreciates many shy and inarticulate boys. It is true that she never will allow any one to be commonplace. She does not know how to come down to a below sea-level atmosphere; she insists on keeping on her fine imaginative plateau and expects people to come up and join her there. Ocassionally, as when a difficult Sunday afternoon tea-party was in progress, this characteristic would embarrass her family.

Portions of the bishop's reminiscences poured out to Mr. Kestell on the sofa now reach the general ear.

'A trek of 300 miles in blazing heat – small, wiry little brown men – sent photographic group to the *Mission Field* – left 100 Bibles.'

'Don't *move*,' says Mrs. Kestell, kindly, but almost imperiously, keeping the bishop on the sofa with a swift hand laid upon his shoulder as she sees the gaitered legs uncrossing to rise and bring her into the conversation. She likes the bishop, but feels instinctively that she will not be able to give her mind to his particular activities; she will only feel absent-minded again. 'The Vice-Provost is so happy there on the sofa with you. I am going down into the garden with Mr. ——.'

Mr. —— is a small colleger, but she always treats all intelligent boys, however young, as though they were men of the world; often, too, as if they possessed a full grasp of French literature, more commonly

72

found in elderly diplomats. She now sits in the garden and reads *Sainte Beuve* aloud to him, beginning in the middle of the book just where she had left her book-marker. It is in a way easier to manage the unwieldy tea-party after Mrs. Kestell has gone; nevertheless, a flatness is immediately felt in the drawing-room when she has left it.

'So fascinating reading to Mr.——,' she says presently on re-entering the room. 'He understands every *nuance.*'

Evelina now whispers to me to come out of the room, and shows me wet, barefoot marks on the floor in the hall, and says that Roderick has told her that he has had an adventure. He had shot the weir in the family canoe; he had been sucked right under the weir and nearly drowned; and the canoe, which had got caught and wedged between two spars, is smashed up.

We go up to his room and find he has changed his clothes and is now calmly working at his essay on Defoe and smoking his pipe.

'Well, hush it up. Get a cloth and take out the foot-marks or they will betray me, and father will be very much annoyed about the canoe – and my adventure happening on Sunday, and all the rest of it; it will all be such a bore. The College waterman who saved me will make enough fuss about it to-morrow.'

We rub out the marks, and much enjoy this adventure of Roderick's on Sunday when life seems to have got stuck in conversation.

In the evening Brahms' sonatas are played. Some listen; others read; all enjoy the release from the social strain of Sunday afternoon.

Maurice Baring carries a lamp out on to the leads,

on which the drawing-room window opens. He and
Mrs. Kestell sit there with a pile of poetry books. He
reads Ronsard to her while every species of moth and
insect in the Thames Valley circles round the lamp.

The Brahms sonata is abruptly stopped by Evelina
bursting into the drawing-room in her nightgown.
Poe's *Tales of Mystery and Imagination* have done
their work. There is 'a sound of flopping or groping
hands or something' in her room, she says, that she
doesn't quite like. The Vice-Provost takes her away
with him upstairs, and stays with her till she goes to
sleep.

Soon Adela and I are also in bed.

'You know it's too preposterous, this going to
Court,' says Adela quite suddenly, from her pillows.

'I am supposed to be going to choose a dress to-
morrow with mother. Think of the expensive trains
about a mile long! "Le Grand Livre" can't stand this
kind of thing, you know. There is *no* sense of pro-
portion in our family. One could do such much nicer
things with the money, and all our decisions are
erratic. It is *utterly* frivolous!'

'Well, why go? I'm *never* going. Well, I suppose
you *must*; it's not worth a scene. Well, anyhow, out
of the immense trains, dresses can be made for
everyone to wear on and on till we're terrifyingly old,
and all living at home, so I daresay it all comes to the
same thing in the end,' I say, sleepily.

But Adela is now secretly engaged to a Cambridge
undergraduate, so this devastating picture of our fortune is wasted on her.

Silence. The old sheep coughs in the meadow
down below. We rustle gently – then sleep.

It was only the Eton Sunday that seemed oppressive. On summer week-days for generations youth seemed to have had free play.

'It is useless in June to preach to us of asceticism. Winter will come round again sure enough,' was all that the boys seemed to be singing in Chapel, for all the words of the hymns. The chestnuts were now in flower; all the trees had undone their parcels of buds and shaken out their light leaves to the sun. The knock of fresh oiled cricket bats was heard everywhere. The asparagus, strawberry, china-rose season was upon us; the green pea season; and the grey and white flannel season. The boys were basking and expanding. Dressed as comfortably as possible, they were passing through the buttercup meadows quivering in the heat of noon, with their towels round their shoulders, to plunge into Cuckoo Weir for a swim; or with their bare legs were stepping gingerly into 'eights' on the river, or warily into little solitary outriggers pushing off into mid-stream as free as savages.

The summer mood was expressed in a great crescendo every year upon the fourth of June by splendid fireworks by the river.

On that evening, with its banks lit up with fairy lamps, the winding Weir Stream gleamed in the dusk like a jewelled snake. Lightly chattering, thousands of spectators sat by the quiet lapping water waiting for darkness. Then many rockets suddenly shot up through the sky with a scream and a sound like the tearing of a sheet, to burst into a shower of stars that died suddenly, heralding the magnificent display of pouring, whirling, fiery gold that lit up the Castle.

After the delicious summer and autumn had gone,

winter and the bitter cold Thames Valley spring came round again in no time, as the hymns had prophesied! On Sundays, enshrouded in a damp mist, the Vice-Provost, crossing the quadrangle to go to Chapel, looked like a ghost in his white surplice. Floods were frequent; influenzas were terrible. In spite of our great coal fires, our vitality was expended in trying to keep warm.

The winter correspondence that accumulated in my mother's bowl on her writing-table seemed to speak of unending discomforts, cold, rheumatism and depression.

'It seems as if everyone were either dead or a distressed governess,' she writes, in a mood of winter dejection.

CHAPTER EIGHT

I WILL not here describe the musical, comfortable, dignified school to which I was now sent. It was a great contrast to 'Marsh', and I was happy there in the delightful friends I made and devoted to its presiding genius. But she, it must be said, was worldly and I never forgot the greatness of the Sisters of Mercy themselves at the rough convent school, and their beautiful Church. Nor will I go into life in prosperous Berlin, all laid out then for the glorification of the Hohenzollerns, where I went with friends for a winter sojourn with Goethe, Heine, Grimm, music, and conscription. We were delighted with the beautiful uniforms and brisk, hard-working young soldiers with daggers at their sides that we saw everywhere, and never thought that each one was in reality as dangerous as a bit of shrapnel.

We thought the great reviews and manœuvres that seemed always taking place were merely delightful spectacles full of colour for everyone's amusement, and we wished we had conscription in England.

I return again to my home. Adela is now a complete young lady: Evelina is a flapper with a pigtail. My hair is twisted into a Grecian knot; skirts wind about my ankles and hamper me. I am full of vague aspirations and questionings as to what I am to do in life; service and sacrifice were the ideals.

We were not 'thwarted', but our parents seemed to

have no other wish for us but that we should flit for ever about their house.

In that, however, it should not be supposed that they favoured feeble lack of self-reliance, or vapid indolence at home. Seriousness and work must always be there, without being much spoken of. The Transcendental and the Traditional were the guidance. But for myself – those foolish virgins of the parable with their lamps flickering feebly! – I saw myself one of them again and again.

Individual enterprise seemed to suit the whole family. At home music was perpetually wafted into the garden through the open windows; as was also the sound of voices reading aloud; or discussing, very youthfully, urgent questions of that day, anxiety about the 'public good' much felt. Choirs, madrigals, orchestras and musical festivals were our communal enthusiasms, to which rushes to catch trains with Novello's yellow and terra-cotta bound scores – Handel, Bach, Mozart – bore witness. Otherwise 'corporate activities' came under the category of 'effort'. They were not natural to us. Social duties at Eton were thought very important by our parents, and also at the Cloisters itself if our visitors were to enjoy staying. Sometimes we all were very bad at entertaining and had social agonies under social silence, or complete inanity.

Literature was my passion but the weakness of my position towards work lay in the fact that I was by nature a born amateur. I liked living with my interesting mother and I liked to do one thing at a time and another thing at another. The word 'amateurish', however, is a word of reproach. So I purchased *The*

OLD WATER COLOUR SKETCH OF WINDSOR
CASTLE FROM THE ETON WEIR STREAM

Englishwoman's Year Book of that day and consulted its list of professions.

Its article on 'The Stage' was emphatically discouraging; the article on 'Sick Nursing' was inspiring. But Adela would have it that I could not do credit to this last, fine, profession. She said I was not strong enough, had not the muscle, and was absent minded, which might be dangerous for patients. She herself had so much good sense that I always respected her judgments.

Though the *Year Book* made mention of every profession that a woman could have to choose from at that time from that of a don to a dustwoman on the rubbish heaps of the Docks, it was clear to my dismay that I was without a vocation.

Under the circumstances I decide to take a drastic line.

'I am going to be a Sanitary Inspector,' I announce to my family. They scream with laughter. My mother gets up from her chair, shovels coals on to the fire, and throws open a window, thinking all the time.

'I am afraid, darling, it is most unlikely that that will come off. You will have to resign yourself always to being an English lady, doing one thing at one time, and another thing at another,' she says very dryly.

I am much annoyed with her, and begin at once to prepare for an examination. But Mrs. Kestell is, alas! a sinister prophetess. I scrape through exams without honours; I am continually deflected from my course and henceforth do 'one thing at one time, and another thing at another.' I hold no brief at all for myself. I wish I had been less social; frivolous, time-wasting.

One of the things I often did at this time was to go and stay with my aunt by marriage, Lady Ritchie, who was Thackeray's daughter.

I can see her at this moment, beautifully fresh in her lace cap, coming down the staircase of her London house in the morning after breakfast, with a few pages of MS. fluttering in her hand. She would tell me to read it over aloud to her by the dining-room fire, then she would dictate a few alterations, put the charming impressionist writing into an envelope, and rapidly address it to Messrs. Smith and Elder. After that, there were plans for the day to be made, and then came the unmaking of plans too impulsively undertaken. A letter is swiftly written to a millionairess to say that, alas! after all she had been rash in saying she could join her in a yachting cruise; she did not feel equal to it; and she would laugh at herself as she sat by the fire for having thought that she ever could impulsively have accepted anything so unsuitable to herself as going on a yachting cruise and undergoing all the fatigues it would involve in her old age and conversation in the wind on deck. Then she must give up a sitting for her portrait next day. Her order has been given to an artist whose talent is almost nil, but who must be helped. 'He hasn't allowed me to look at my picture yet, but I see him squeezing piles of vermilion on to his palette, and I quite dread it,' and she posts a cheque to the painter.

Very soon after we are whirling away in a little victoria in the morning sunshine. An old lady who has lost her husband must be visited; and all in a moment Aunt Anny has alighted in Queen's Gate, and is sitting in a heavy *early* Victorian dining-room (our dining-rooms, remember, were 'mid' at this time), under an East India Company member's portrait, among the massive mahogany chairs, encouraging and improving the old lady's spirits. The canary begins to sing. A gaunt, depressed daughter, with red hands in mittens, as she arranges the roses we have brought, shows signs of cheering up. Whether the pair subside into dankness after Aunt Anny's departure I do not know, but her presence has been like sun flooding into their gloomy room for the moment.

We whirl on and leave a hobbyhorse and some dolls with the coachman's children who have had the measles. We converse with their mother at the top of a stair in a mews. Other children playing about the mews stop in their play, arrested by my aunt's charming voice as she comes down the stairs to greet them.

We drive on to Westminster, and the victoria stops in Dean's Yard. And now Aunt Anny begins to feel nervous and anxious about the 'odd little errand' upon which we are going. She has an appointment with the Dean, and he is ready for us: he leads us through his house and on in to the Abbey and down into the crypt. There we find in an alcove Onslow Ford, the sculptor, also his assistant, and the bust of William Thackeray that has been moved there by them from its niche in Poets' Corner.

The fact is for years, whenever she has been to Westminster Abbey, Aunt Anny has deplored the length of the whiskers on each side of the face of her father's bust. The Italian sculptor, Marachetti, made them too long. They spoil the likeness for her and she has longed to have them clipped, and so at last she has begged Onslow Ford, and has implored the Dean to

81

let her have her wish, and have them shortened. So now chip, chip, chip fly the bits under the white-bloused assistant's chisel. Sir Onslow Ford stands by, very cross, for he does not like undoing another sculptor's work, and if the daughter of Thackeray had not happened to be such a charming old lady, it is probable she would not have had her way. She laughs, admits that there is something absurd about the commission, but is firm that it shall be carried out; so she talks to him without paying any attention to his crossness, and makes him at last smile as he superintends the work. Finally the bust is flicked over with a cloth, as after a shave, and it is carried up into the nave and back into its own niche, and the silence and dignity of the Abbey received it again. We all survey the bust in silence, and then disperse.

Aunt Anny is a little emotional as she gets into the victoria, smiling at her tears, then weeping again; she is triumphant, for it has been a great relief to her mind.

Her wit was so lightly lambent that often people missed her points. Samuel Butler went to call upon her one day soon after his *Authoress of the Odyssey* (which insists that that book was written by a woman) had been published. He told her he was at work on a book on Shakespeare's sonnets. He was, however, only bewildered at her saying, 'Oh, Mr. Butler, do you know my theory about the sonnets? They were written by Anne Hathaway to Shakespeare!' It was not she who repeated this story, but the author of *Erewhon*. He never saw that she was laughing at him, and used to tell it, shaking his head sadly and saying, 'Poor lady, that was a silly thing to say.'

CHAPTER NINE

FOR some years now, after Adela and I had left the schoolroom, it had been our custom to spend the end of the season in London. This came about every year because the wife of a Colonel in the Guards persuaded my mother to let her occupy our house at Eton, while she lent us her house in London.

'So good for sweet Adela and Mary to have a little fling? So good for darling Evelina's lessons?' reads my mother from the persuasive Mrs. Darcy's letter.

'And so good for Mrs. Darcy to have the river, the garden, and the library,' adds the Vice-Provost a little tartly over the rim of the *Times*.

Once more the four-wheeler piled with luggage has brought us away from Paddington and turned into the eighteenth-century square, as into a hushed cove, out of the roaring sea of Oxford Street. We alight at Mrs. Darcy's house. My mother is at once perfectly happy in the drawing-room with its long mirrors and Bühl furniture, where at a great escritoire she seats herself and writes imaginative letters telling her friends where to come and find her.

But Mr. Kestell sits in the over-furnished boudoir with Adela, Mary, and Evelina, and they all grumble together in the drowsy afternoon heat, surrounded on all sides with Adonises of the Guards in silver frames, which presently they will put away.

'The Colonel, you may be sure, doesn't like my study, and I don't like his,' says Mr. Kestell. He has thrown one knee over the other and is shaking his foot impatiently. 'It's a mere tank, for his racing calendar and spurs; and there is a stale smell of cat rising up from the pavement.'

'Mother is probably writing a letter upstairs saying that the Vice-Provost is as happy as a king in the Colonel's study,' says Adela drowsily.

'And Mrs. Darcy is probably writing a letter saying that the Colonel is as happy as a king in Mr. Kestell's dear, delightful, dowdy study,' Mary suggests.

'No – dear, delightful, dowdy Mr. Kestell's study,' suggests Evelina.

'You see, father, it was exceedingly tiresome of you to submit to the exchange again this year,' she adds, throwing her arms round the Vice-Provost's neck.

'Oh, well, your mother does so much enjoy London, and it is really useful to me to be at the British Museum every day just now, I must remember. You will enjoy your season.'

'Oh, no, father, we shall not for a single moment. We have no clothes – we are dowdy. Nothing could satisfy me but to be simply tremendously smart and dash round the Park, driving a barouche and pair with a tiger on the back seat,' says Mary fiercely, a swift vision of a totally unattainable elegance darting into her head.

Adela then grumbles too. 'Yes, and just look at our engagements. The Archbishop's Garden Party and then the Bishop's Garden Party. Old Sir Theodore's jaunt, and then there's that hop at Lady A's. She only knows about twelve young men – all under life-size or with squints.'

'This is *absurd*,' says Mr. Kestell. 'You want me to exclaim over and over again like Mrs. Allen, when she took Catherine Morland to Bath: "If only we had some acquaintance here!" As a matter of fact you know perfectly well that lots of fun will crop up, and before you know where you are, you are in a whirl of most delightful parties, my dear children,' says Mr. Kestell, thinking that the grumbling must really cease.

But Mary goes on querulously. 'Then the awful shopping. Everything lovely – too expensive – dying of heat in shops, and coming out with nothing but a nervous breakdown!'

'My dear, my dear! Your father ought to have had ten thousand a year at least. You must be *good*!' says Mr. Kestell.

'Mary, you adore shopping,' says Adela quietly.

We have all been rather like babies waking up from sleep and wailing at absolutely nothing. But it is a thundery, stifling afternoon. After some fragrant tea out of Mrs. Darcy's Crown Derby, we feel refreshed, and soon our mood completely changes. We see Mr. Kestell off affectionately, at the front door, in his scholarly black morning-coat, and Ruskinian-blue tie drawn through a ring. Though he will only be out until the evening, we all embrace him as if he were going on a far journey; and though we have all just spent some hours together he wishes to know exactly when he is to see us all again.

'Remember we shall spend a great deal of money on clothes when we go out,' says Adela.

'Yes, you will be punished for bringing us here by our extravagance,' Mary says with a Goneril-like thrust at the last.

'No, no, no. Poor, but clean. Poor, but clean,' and he runs down the steps and disappears down the street. He may be going to the London Library to look up some point for the book on Medieval Chivalry that he is writing, or to look in at Sotheby's to see some Elzevirs that he feels with pain will certainly be bought for America; then he will probably call on an old lady at St. James's Palace; or visit the Athenæum where he will hide behind pillars from other old gentlemen; or hear an anthem at the Abbey before he has finished his day.

Adela and I in the late afternoon stroll through Hanover Square and Bond Street, tantalized as we flatten our noses abstemiously in the 'street of elegant shops'. We both adore shoes, hats, and gowns. Then we jingle down to Knightsbridge in a hansom, and here we flatten again, and then make a self-indulgent plunge inside. We buy green shoes, to wear with white muslin Sir Joshua dresses.

'Cleanliness *can't* be combined with poverty,' says Adela, remembering Mr. Kestell's injunctions, among billows of flowered chiffon.

'No, I know, it's impossible,' says Mary, and she pounces upon white silk stockings to wear with green shoes. In the end we spend a great deal, and everything is put down to Mrs. Kestell's account. It is 'feast' not 'fast' just now. 'Le Grand Livre' will lie in its drawer for many a day after the exchange of houses with Mrs. Darcy, for no one will have the courage to bring it out.

That evening, Mrs. Kestell at her writing-table is writing to one of her friends:

'Adela and Mary are off, radiant, to their dance,

looking like flowers in their calyxes, with their sweet young faces; in their white and green.'

'Why *do* they say these things to each other?' says Adela in the hansom trotting across the Park to the dance at Mrs. Tallboys' on Campden Hill. She has just repeated the words that she read over her mother's shoulder to Mary and Mr. Fitzgerald, who is accompanying them to the dance, and peals of laughter have floated out of the hansom into the summer dusk.

'Which part of you is the calyx, do you suppose?' says Fitzgerald, leading out over the hansom doors,* enjoying the girls' conversation and his cigarette.

The latter is our greatest friend. We cannot do without him. He seems to have unlimited time, and though he strolls through life as if it were a vast exhibition, at any booth of which he can tarry as long as it pleases his fancy, he never appears in the least demoralised by leisure; though there are grave head-shakings over his 'career.' Everyone may be concerned about him, but he quietly goes his own way.

He seems to set our minds free from the pressure of social primness of the outer circle at Eton. We are natural and happy with him as he takes us round with him, making a diverting Lord George Sanger-like show for us out of social London, by his subtle observation, his humane humour, and his detachment.

And now we are trip-clip-clopping, trip-clip-clopping up through the leafy bowers of Campden Hill, and stop at a tall Norman-Shaw architected house—alight, and pass through marble, up marble, through

* You might go three in a hansom to a dance. You did not go alone with a partner to a dance, or come home with a partner alone.

a close conglomeration of Italian shrines, caskets, cabinets, marqueterie; against the tangled background of William Morris's pomegranates; past the pictures by Rossetti, Sir Frederic Leighton, Burne-Jones, Holman Hunt, and Mr. Watts, of which the host is the renowned possessor. On and across the parquet floor to the fascinating, artistic, gracious hostess, and to the massive, comfortable chaperons in their rich waisted velvets and long trains, seated in formidable yet customary array.

We have dance programmes given us, on which is printed only one word, 'Valse,' all the way down, interspersed twice with the word 'Lancers.' Soon, in our shimmering white or pink satins, with our long white kid gloves, elegant waists and sprays of flowers on the left side of our bodices, our hair coiled on the nape of our necks or on the top of our heads, our trains first swirling about our feet, then gracefully caught up and managed, we fall with our partners into the swinging rhythm of that old 'Blue Danube' Valse.

Duennas and chaperons were fast going out even at that date; but at this house many lorgnons still bristled, and elderly heads nodded together over the young things whirling round the centre of the room; for Mrs. Tallboys had a passion for young people, and invited her eminent contemporaries to come and watch them as though they were a lot of young sea-lions plunging about, at whom it was a great pleasure to look. Thus many of her friends would come and look on, diverted by the antics of the young creatures and secretly prognosticating mating. We were used to this. Had the phalanx been a dull one it would have been depressing, but as a matter of fact

88

the fine vitality of the elderly and eminent, both male and female, of Mrs. Tallboys' acquaintance, gave a certain spice to the dances in her house. She had a particular atmosphere and 'tenue' of her own.

Over one's partner's shoulder one would see, for instance, that Mr. Henry James had come in. A few more whirls round, and one has a glimpse at his face, which betrays that nervous suffering which a sense of shortcomings of words was apt to throw him into at any moment. It was an artist's agitation carried to an extreme over possible failure in expressing his fine and complicated idea; a hesitation that postponed the moment when he must eventually let the inadequate little phrase pass from between his lips at a run, since his listener waited.

At the amusing phrase at last chosen the hostess would throw back her head a moment, laughing, and then perhaps she carried him off to look at a Corot or Whistler in the next room.

Another round of the long Valse and one perceives that old Herr Joachim and his quartette have come in after a concert, and Mrs. Tallboys takes him down to the dining-room to sup with the *élite* of his English musical circle of adorers.

One steps with a little more freedom for the absence of the elderly and eminent. Many members of the younger generation of this circle, 'faithless and perverse' just like any other generation, wanted to get out of the atmosphere in which they were brought up. This seems to be a general rule and not confined to any particular generation; and it is no conclusive criticism of the receding period. Our elders, after all, had won all their refined and graceful art and sounded the high, noble note of poetry and symbolism, through rebellion against Philistine ugliness and the narrow terrors of an outworn evangelical creed. And now here were many contrary young creatures already feeling they were simmering in a syrup. They were just beginning to seek for fresh values, telling each other that they were stifled by emphatic and misty gush and 'couleur de rose' rapture. But at present there was only a dissatisfied groping for fresh expression.

The arrogance which perhaps became a necessity of self-assertion for a while, and has been a decided characteristic of the first twenty years of the twentieth century, had not yet come into fashion – piquant in a very few, vile in the pretentious. Some bold and definite spirits of this set had already declared they wouldn't have their roots growing in drawing-room flower-pots any longer; they were all for 'Beachcombing,' whatever that might mean; just a few disappeared. Count Tolstoi was beginning to make a profound disturbance with his exposition of Christianity. Since the Great War many people have found it easy enough to turn a fork in a potato patch, from choice or necessity; but even Count Tolstoi himself, as a pioneer, in the nineteenth century found himself baulked by his wife's gardeners—so the difficulties of these young rebels can be imagined. Tolstoi's youthful followers were many, but they were all baffled by the ease, comfort, and established order of the nineteenth century. Many young women, intending to become artists and writers, were beginning to feel the need of opportunities and independence. In contrast, however, to such tentative seekers, there were also a number of young Philistines among the dancers, who thought all the future artists, poets, men of letters of this circle, outsiders. They were intending themselves to find a more conventional set as soon as possible, having a great respect for will-power, but a horror of the Imagination.

But I am not thinking, of course, of these things in the whirl of the Valse. The Joachim quartette have by this time demolished several cold fowls and boot-shaped glazed tongues, and it is time for the dancers to swarm down to the dining-room.

And now, at this distance of time, I hear a faint popping of corks, and laughter at the 'flash' of talk that passes across the little supper-tables in the tapestried room; I remember rapid exchanges of confidences with intimate cousins; a light tap with a fan on my shoulder draws my attention. I feel the absorption of happy lovers, or the hidden tragedies of men loving and not loved, or of young girls loving and not loved; sentimental Valse music tearing at their hearts.

The bright trivial animation of the ball-room I cannot reproduce. I feel it is muffled now, faded, and ghostly.

Once when I passed with my children by the door of Mrs. Tallboys' high house, I suddenly remembered a spring afternoon when a famous singer at the piano carolled, as though one with the nightingales and thrushes, in the romantic manner so abandonedly enjoyed by her nineteenth-century audience, who as they listened then were gazing vaguely out among the leaves and spreading branches of the great chestnut tree in the Square garden.

'Wait one minute! The house we are passing is full of ghosts to me,' I said to the children. They attended for a second with their ball lifted – then thought better of hearing me out – threw their ball before them and ran off.

So I never speak of my memories as I pass the house now, with whomever I may be; I know I shall not be able adequately to reanimate the shades, and shall only be a bore. But in silence, and just for myself, I like to pass again in mind through the door and up the marble stairs, and find Mrs. Tallboys among her cabinets and damask, with Mr. Henry James, and all her idealistic, romantic, highly sophisticated, delicate-minded contemporaries.

When her dance is over, 'Who were the blots?' Mrs. Tallboys asks an intimate friend as she comes back into her emptied room, having said good night to most of her guests. Though gracious and romantic, Mrs. Tallboys is also satirical.

Adela and I, animated and still a little out of breath after the last extra, get into our hansom and wave good night to Fitzgerald.

As the horse trots gently through the London dawn, we begin to yawn and feel a great fatigue; then we lie back in our corners silent; two puppets limp on their strings after the drama is ended.

CHAPTER TEN

AND then one pale February morning we woke to see
from our windows that the Royal Standard was flying
at half-mast. Queen Victoria was dead. It seemed un-
believable.

My mother, looking out of a window above her
writing-table, upon the full stretch of Windsor Castle,
wrote in her diary: 'The winter evening is closing in
with blue vapours and stillness; the wooded slopes
embowering and fringing the Castle look like blue
smoke, but overhead the sky is clear and luminous;
the towers spring proudly above the fog; and upon
the topmost roof to-day – heartbreakingly – waves
the banner half-mast high, *for the Queen*! The great
alders on one side of the Thames hold up their bare
arms in the foreground; this evening, when all
things have one significance, they look like the arms
of mourners held up to heaven, motionless, bereft.

'The pathos of the end of the Victorian age is not
to be embodied in any immediate manifestation. But
this day of mourning at the Castle is full of still
beauty.'

Evelina and I are to go to Windsor for the funeral.

'Oh, father, it is too lovely having mourning without any grief,' exclaims Evelina, looking at herself
in the drawing-room mirror in an inexpensive, but
captivating, black coat and skirt. She felt what every
woman in England felt. All had been delightfully

93

occupied in getting themselves into histrionic and becoming black for three whole days.

'It will be a very good procession, father, don't you think? I mean, as history goes. As about as important as the Field of the Cloth of Gold, don't you think?' says Mary stupidly, also now looking at herself in the glass.

'Oh, Mary, how you must always analyse and classify everything. She's always in Little Arthur's *History of England*,' says Evelina.

'Well, everything is *very* like it,' Mary says in self-defence.

'Mary is very elementary,' says my mother, severely.

'Not at all,' my father defends me. 'She likes to get things clear, and has a feeling for elementary history, that's all.'

'You look perfectly radiant, darling children, in your black,' says my mother.

'Well, we'll compose ourselves when we get up to Windsor. We really ought to be off,' says Mary, and she draws on black suède gloves with a smile of pleasure.

Our parents, on each side of the fire, discuss the question as to who will preach to the boys the *oraison funèbre* that must be given in chapel.

Meanwhile, Evelina and I, over near the window, indulge in a rapid and silent funeral charade as we put on our gloves.

Queen Victoria had been familiar to us from earliest childhood, and now we were sorry that we should never again, for the enlivement of our walks in Datchet Lane or thereabouts, suddenly see the outrider on his dapple grey, in his white buckskin breeches, shoot into sight, heralding the approach of the Queen, and we should never again drop our curtseys at the moment when the great landau bounced her forward for her bow, as she drove past us behind her white horses with her Indian servant on the box.

But it is not possible that at this stage of our lives we should feel 'the pathos of the end of the Victorian age.' The death of a very ancient queen provides a unique occasion in our life for the frivolous enjoyment of our coal-black mourning.

For a second I claw at Evelina's shoulder with the mien of an ancient hag entering a death chamber; for a second she expresses funeral emotion with a white handkerchief and black hands, outspread over her face as she rocks to and fro. We instantly desist but the Vice-Provost and Mrs. Kestell have seen and reprove us for our frivolity. It is time to be off. We extend demon hands for a warm at the fire. Then we embrace our parents and depart.

When we reach Windsor we are met at the door of one of the towers of the Castle by the wife of an equerry. She seems genuinely emotional, and she mounts the towers sorrowfully like a Madame Mal-brook. We follow her up the stairs and out to the battlements, falling in with her sober mood.

There are many black-clad guests assembled there. The equerry's wife is, of course, not giving a party on this occasion, but she has remembered that many friends from Windsor and Eton will like to be present, and so she has invited them to come to her tower. We are to stay on the top of the tower for a while to see the Windsor contingent of English chivalry gathering for the final procession to Henry VII's Chapel. This will take place on the arrival of the Queen's coffin from London; for another great pageant-like procession is winding round the capital first, for the people of England.

At first we see nothing at all from the tower. Then a few beetle-black, top-hatted and frock-coated, humble relations of the Queen hurry across the space below.

'Field of the Cloth of God!' whispers Evelina to me mockingly.

Presently, down below, from the door of another tower, comes Alexandra, whom we still call the Princess of Wales, gracefully shrouded in a long black veil, followed by the German Emperor in eagled helmet.

Two upholsterers caught, unprepared, with a great roll of red carpet, bow and hesitate and fumble right in their way, in confusion at not having got the thing down in time for royal feet. The Emperor seizes the roll, straightens it, kicks it with his spurred boot, and set the red flannel path running down the slope of the square towards the chapel for Alexandra to walk on. He looks romantic, alert, and handsome. The upholsterers rush ignominiously down after their carpet to deal with it at the other end.

The Emperor is clearly going to see for himself that all is arranged as it should be in Henry VII's Chapel.

It grows desperately cold in the airy regions up on the tower. A mist hangs over the river, and all distances are obscured. The guests decide to withdraw

96

from the battlements. We file down the narrow staircase inside the tower. In the equerry's drawing-room we all thaw, expand, and glow in the warmth, and are regaled by a butler with hot lemonade and frivolous-looking bon-bons and *foie gras* in filigree silver, incongruously festive against the heavy mourning of the guests.

Conversation is difficult. The charming wife of the equerry and her daughters are sad, and as this is their house into which we have all trooped, none wish to be frivolous like the *foie gras*; or, on the other hand, too heavily funereal like our clothes. A *via media* of dignified gloom, however, is somehow found as the guests warm themselves and wait. The hostess is feeling quite worn out, for a state of hurry and bustle has reigned in Windsor such as reigns before private theatricals, and she still now keeps going in and out of the room, fulfilling duties for her husband connected with the death of the Queen.

Royal weddings, jubilees, and coronations can be dealt with by rehearsal and preparation: funerals must be impromptu. All European princes and governors, or their representatives who were coming, had to be put up and fed with 'funeral bakemeats,' and their suites put up and fed. All England had had to be instructed how to behave and what to wear. There were hardly any telephones and very few motors: everything was regulated, let us say, at landau and pair speed. Thus all was confusion in the Castle.

Presently one of the daughters of the house, with a key in her hand, leads us all down by steps into a garden and round to the swards, which slope from the Castle down to the Long Walk. The Eton boys

97

H

are assembled here for a splendid view, and we take up our stand among them. It grows very late. The cold is intense. At last the great procession turns in at the Long Walk and comes on uphill towards us.

Men have been half-frozen waiting at the station, and the artillery horses that were to have drawn the gun-carriage bearing the coffin, have jibbed and fretted. The gunners, in a state of tension in the cold (though doing a perfectly easy thing on horses that they know), had grown so nervous themselves at last with the incessant fidgeting, that they finally imparted their own nerves to the horses, who then became totally unmanageable.

There was nothing for it but to take the horses out of harness, and now we see that sailors with their gaiters and jolly red necks and blue collars are coming on up the hill, drawing the gun-carriage with the coffin placed upon it. We are crying with the emotion set up by the solemn drums, on which the heralds on milk-white steeds are drubbing. The rooks are all flying about over the Castle, flapping slow, slow, and cawing in a disturbed state high above the battlements. The splendid procession with its kings and princes from all over the world passes us close, through the Castle gate-way; then it winds on its way to the Norman archway, and to Henry VII's Chapel. It is lost from our view.

Queen Victoria's endlessly long, deliciously quiet reign is over.

'We all caught chills at the Queen's funer—'

'No, Mary! Do not go on in this prating way! The last sentence before that was the best one with which to end the book. You have already gone beyond the

98

boundary set by the title,' says one half of myself to the other.

'But it is always possible to make out that childhood only ends where second childishness begins; and then one could go on for a long while,' says the other half.

'Do not be silly! and you know when we planned out the short sketch how we resolved not to go into deep troubles, love, bereavements, marriage, childbirth, and above all the Great War. We should be out of our depth in a moment, and you know neither of us can swim.'

'And is not a single skeleton to be brought out of the cupboard?'

'No, not one skeleton!'

'How dull. However, just as you wish.'

We are one again; and now that that is so, I will not stay longer than to tell how, a year after the death of the Queen, we used to see Windsor Castle blazing with lights at night as we had never seen it before. Ever since Fanny Burney held pins for Queen Charlotte's toilet in one of the recesses of those windows, and George III was offering his gentlemen-in-waiting a little barley-water by way of refreshment after hunting, until the day Queen Victoria died, the note of Windsor had been a subdued one.

'The chandeliers of the state apartments have been shrouded in great white bags too long,' thought Edward VII when he came to the throne; and he had the rooms all lit up and gave some festive parties.

It is on a flat note that one may end up a sketch of a quiet nineteenth-century childhood, and now I am glad the little book is finished, for I do not want to become one of those who only live with departed shades and quiet memories. I want to live in the present.

But sometimes how pleasant it is to unlock the casket of memories and rummage among the things put away in it; and then, how I love to hear the College clock clanging out the hour of hot noon; to think of the secluded creek with its swift-running water and border of willows; to think of sitting with my beloved mother, with windows open to the summer night, hearing in the silence the gentle stir of the tall poplar tree, and the romantic sounding of 'the Last Post.'